IØ142543

My Journey With The Queen Of Peace: 28 Days In
Medjugorje

Copyright © 2019 Jose De Santiago

All rights reserved. No part of this publication may be
reproduced, stored in a retrieval system, or
transmitted, in any form or in any means – by
electronic, mechanical, photocopying, recording or
otherwise – without prior written permission, except as
permitted by U.S. copyright law.

(De Santiago Family Publishing)
ISBN-13:978-0-578-55150-0

For The Queen of Peace

Table of Contents

Introduction

This book is an account of my twenty-eight days in Medjugorje, this small village in Bosnia-Herzegovina. My first pilgrimage, which was only one week, was in March of 2018 and my second pilgrimage was in February-March 2019, which was for three weeks. The pilgrimage of March of 2018, marked a new beginning, so to speak, in this supernatural journey the Lord God had set me on which started back in 2006. An account of that testimony are in my two previous books *My Life in the Supernatural: A Story of Divine Mercy and My Life in the Supernatural: A Story of Divine Mercy-Volume 2*.

The Spiritual Gifts and Charisms described in those books play a big part in what occurred during my twenty-eight total days in Medjugorje. Those familiar with these supernatural gifts will understand what unfolded during these pilgrimages.

The First Chapter *Medjugorje* of this book is duplicate of Chapter Twelve of my second book *Volume 2*. This will give an account to the reader on what occurred during my first pilgrimage in 2018. This First Chapter sets up the remainder of this book.

My hopes with this book are to help spread the Messages of Medjugorje to the World and to give testimony to Our Lord and to Our Lady's miracles.

Chapter 1: Medjugorje 2018

On June 24, 1981, the apparitions of the Blessed Virgin Mary began in a small village in Bosnia and Herzegovina, which is part of the former Yugoslavia.

Our Lady appeared to six children in this unknown village on a rocky steep hill and has delivered numerous messages to the visionaries over these many years.

Medjugorje has received more than it's fair share of criticism over the years. Everything from it being a hoax, to it being a diabolical manifestation.

My first knowledge of the tiny place in South Central Europe was in the 1980's. There were several TV specials during the early years of the apparitions which I remember watching. I know my parents and my sisters were interested in them. My parents even had some Holy Water given to them from Medjugorje in the 1980's. I remember taken some unbeknownst to them and blessing myself with it.

I didn't think too much about Medjugorje after that until my conversion began in 2006.

The advent of the Internet in the 1990's gave the world access to this remote holy place. The apparition events, the moment the visionaries *saw* the Holy Virgin, were recorded and were ready to be played to anyone who wished to view them via the World Wide Web.

I became very curious about these apparition events after my own supernatural path began to unfold in 2006.

Most of the videos I would watch were that of Mirjana Soldo, one of the six visionaries. Mirjana receives monthly apparitions on the 2nd of every month and on every March 18th which also happens to be Mirjana's birthday.

Her daily apparitions stopped after eighteen months, which began in 1981.

Our Lady wished for these monthly messages to be for those who do not yet know the love of God.

I watched many videos of the apparitions over the years to see if I could *feel* anything at the moment Our Lady *appeared* to Mirjana. I figured I would be able to sense something to confirm to me that she was really appearing in Medjugorje.

I honestly never really sensed anything during these recorded events. That didn't mean that she wasn't appearing there, it just meant that I wasn't *given* the grace to *sense* it in this way. Yet one of her monthly apparitions did confirm a message I *received* from Our Lady back in 2008.

My first intention or aspiration to make a pilgrimage to Medjugorje was in 2012. There was pilgrimage scheduled for the Spring of 2012 by the pilgrimage company we used for our first pilgrimage in 2008 to France. One of the stops in this particular pilgrimage in 2012 was to Medjugorje. I believe it was going to be just a two-day stop there. Nevertheless I wanted to go.

My oldest sister Maria was diagnosed with breast cancer in January of 2012 and her subsequent surgery in February prevented us from going. I made a personal offering to Our Lady in hopes of making that trip. My prayers were answered, but it took six years for it to come to pass.

In those six years, my belief that Our Lady was appearing there was met with doubt. Many stories, reports and commentaries against these apparitions appeared online over the years as well. My reading them allowed doubt to come in.

I really wanted to believe it was true but some of these so-called reports made a good case that it was false. Reporting false facts and claims can strengthen any case if the person trying to determine the validity of a something is debating a certain claim, and in my case the Medjugorje apparitions.

In March of 2017, I made a pilgrimage with my parents and a niece and nephew to Fatima, Portugal for the 100th anniversary of Our Lady appearing to three children in 1917. Fatima is an official Catholic Church approved Marian apparition site and as of this writing, Medjugorje is not. It's still under Church investigation but all signs are pointing that it will be an official Marian apparition site.

In the midst of this pilgrimage I asked the priest who was traveling with us about a recent five-part social media report against Medjugorje that I was reading. His response caught me off guard. I was expecting him to agree with this report for some reason. He said, "if someone says that they see the Holy Mother, who are we to say it's not true". This made a lot of sense to me.

Through my own experiences, people have questioned what I have "received" even though I know with all my heart what I *saw* and *heard* was from God or from Our Lady.

In November of 2016, a month after my brother's passing, my parents and I and two of my nephews, made a two-hour drive North from our hometown to a see documentary on Medjugorje called "Apparition Hill".

Apparition Hill, which was filmed in 2015, brought together seven people of different backgrounds and beliefs. There was a widower, a woman with terminal cancer, a drug addict, a man with ALS, two atheists, and a woman who struggled with accepting the Church's teaching of Our Lady.

This film was extraordinary. I won't go into any detail about it here. I hope you all will see it for yourselves. It truly is an incredible and inspiring film.

The desire to visit Medjugorje increased after that, and even more so after purchasing the DVD later and viewing it several more times. I made contact with one of the filmmakers, Cimela Kidonakis, via social media. Cimela actually submitted a video entry when the Film Company was asking for video submissions on why they should be chosen to go to Medjugorje. The chosen winners, had a two-week pilgrimage to Medjugorje paid for in order to make this documentary.

She was asked to join the filmmaking process by the director Sean Bloomfield, after her submission wasn't chosen. Cimela has her own production company that is based out of Houston, Texas and Sean was impressed by her work.

I was in contact with Cimela for about a year when the opportunity for me to make this pilgrimage came to pass.

Her passion for Medjugorje played a key role in my decision to make this long awaited pilgrimage to this small village in Europe.

The filmmakers of *Apparition Hill* also lead pilgrimages to Medjugorje.

One of the incredible blessings of these pilgrimages that they offer was staying at the pansion, which is sort of a guesthouse, of one of the six original seers, Mirjana Soldo.

I very quickly, by the strong calling of Our Lady, was able to book the trip for mid-March of 2018. The trip included being able to be present at Mirjana's annual apparition of March 18th. Like I mentioned before, the 18th of March also happened to be Mirjana's birthday. This particular pilgrimage was called *My Heart Will Triumph*. It is from Mirjana's title of her first book, an autobiographical account of her life including the incredible insight of a life of a visionary.

After reading Mirjana's book, I was 100% sure that she was totally genuine. Her words erased any lingering doubt that may have been floating around at this point.

I spiritually prepared a few weeks before the trip to be ready for whatever Our Lord and Our Lady had prepared for the group and myself.

The opportunity to meet Mirjana was definitely one of the things I was most looking forward to. Reading her words made feel a connection with her. I felt as though she was an old friend by the time I reached the end of the book.

It felt as though it was a dream as the days leading up to trip quickly passed. I couldn't believe I was actually traveling to Medjugorje!

After a long travel day, our little group of fourteen pilgrims arrived in this small village in Bosnia and Herzegovina.

We had pilgrims from California, Florida, Wisconsin and New York and other states. I was the only Texan there aside from Cimela, who hadn't arrived yet.

After an early dinner in our pansion, which is run by Mirjana and her husband Marko, our group leader, Erin Pynes, invited some of us to go climb Apparition Hill where The Queen of Peace first appeared in June of 1981.

It was already dark by the time we made the climb up the rocky hill to the spot where Our Lady first appeared. It had rained by the time we got to Medjugorje and that made the climb a little rough. We used lights from our cell phones to light our way the steep hill. It was an incredible sight to see what I had only seen in pictures and videos, the spot where the Mother of God appeared to six children thirty-seven years ago! We all prayed for a bit before we headed down for night.

The next morning at breakfast was the first time I spotted Mirjana Soldo. She was helping serve breakfast to the pilgrims. She only came out briefly a couple of times and she didn't speak to any of us. There were only around twenty-five to thirty people there. There was a second group there who joined us through some part of our stay and activities there in Medjugorje.

The daily schedule in Medjugorje usually consists of daily Mass in English in the chapel just outside St James Church. They have other daily masses in different language before and after the English Mass. The evening prayer program begins at 5pm everyday. One of the visionaries said it was Our Lady who requested this. Right before the evening program begins, they have adoration in the chapel from 2-5pm.

The evening program begins with the Sacrament of Reconciliation right at 5pm. There is a long row of outdoor confessional boxes right outside the church to accommodate the many pilgrims from around the world. The many priests, who come here from all over the world as well, are the ones who hear the confessions. The pilgrims just line up in whatever language is available at the time. During the same 5 o'clock hour, the Holy Rosary is being recited inside St. James Church, which is the main Church in Medjugorje. Ten decades of the Rosary are prayed before the 6 o'clock International Mass begins. At 5:40pm, everything stops as Our Lady comes. She still appears to three of the visionaries daily but in private most of the time now. The church bells ring at that hour and silent prayer is said. The Rosary then continues. After the International Mass, another five decades of the Rosary is prayed along with some other prayers.

A Holy Hour of Adoration is also held several times a week in the Church. It's takes place right after the International Mass at times or a little later from 9pm-10pm.

Daily spiritual talks are also given to the pilgrims throughout the day in a large hall behind St. James. Our group attended two talks during our stay, which were inspiring and informative.

One of the talks was from a Dominican priest named Father Leon, who also appeared in the documentary *Apparition Hill*. He spoke about his own experience of an apparition of Our Lady when he was twenty-years old. He experienced it when he was a soldier and came on pilgrimage to Medjugorje. I will leave his testimony for the future pilgrim to hear.

Our local guide was Miki Musa. He also appeared in *Apparition Hill*. He is the one who writes down Our Lady's message to Mirjana as soon as the apparition ends. Mirjana then gives the message to Miki who quickly gives a rough translation to the pilgrims gathered. The full message in its final translation is given later in the day in multiple languages.

Miki is an incredible guide. He was nine-years old when the apparitions began. He is a very good friend of Mirjana and is very knowledgeable on the history of Medjugorje. He gave us a talk as well. He is very enthusiastic about his faith and is very genuine as well.

He led us up Apparition Hill on our second day of pilgrimage. There are fifteen huge stone markers up and down the hill marking the fifteen Mysteries of the Rosary. The final five, the Luminous Mysteries, are behind St. James Church. We prayed the Rosary as we made our climb. We stopped at the stone markers and Miki reflected on that particular mystery. It was a very spiritual experience. We then all had plenty of time to pray on our own as we reached the top of the apparition site.

I went to Confession later when the evening program began. I went to an American priest who had received the gift of *Reading of Souls.* Pilgrims will encounter many priests with incredible Charisms of the Holy Spirit in Medjugorje. I was anxiously waited for about an hour before it was my turn. In reading about St. Padre Pio who is well known for this particular gift, I was anticipating being *told* something from this American priest.

I'm incredibly grateful that I was able to take part in the Sacrament of Reconciliation in Medjugorje, which is often referred as the *Confessional of the World* but I was disappointed in a way as well. My hopes to have *received* something from this priest with this particular gift didn't come to pass. It just wasn't the will of the Lord.

I then went to Mass in the incredibly packed St. James Church. I was standing right at the main exit by the one of the doors. It was cold and so I was able to keep a little warm by standing just inside the one closed door. After Mass, Adoration began. I was able to find some of my group and we made our way to the area right in front of the pews. We had an incredible seat in adoring Our Lord ever present in the Holy Eucharist. It was an incredible hour of prayer and adoration. I prayed for everyone who asked me to pray for them before I embarked on my trip. The atmosphere was incredible but the *effect* did not hit me until the middle of night. The openness of my soul during the Holy Hour allowed many things to come in.

As I explained in my first book and in this one about this *Supernatural Empathic Gift* I was given, I became a magnet to the pain, hurt and suffering and other emotions of all the pilgrims that were there adoring Our Lord. Some of the group and myself went out to dinner afterwards and so whatever I *received*, didn't manifest itself until my soul was quiet and that was the middle of night while I was in bed.

This deep pain within my soul awakened me, which brought me to tears. I was given to *know* what it was I was *feeling*. It was the deep pains that the pilgrims brought with them that night. These pains were of family, health and spiritual problems. I could *feel* and *hear* them crying out to Our Lord. I could *see* them as though I was still present there at St. James. I could *hear* the words "why am I here!" over and over. It even came out of my mouth as though it was my own thought. It was a rough night after that. I didn't sleep much and by the time breakfast came around, the *pain* was still lingering. I felt awful. I explained to Erin, our leader, what I had *experienced*. She and her friend Leigh, who was on her second pilgrimage to Medjugorje, were incredibly sympathetic and understanding to what I *experienced* on this pilgrimage. I'm very thankful to them. The rest of the group was also very kind and loving. I couldn't have asked for a better group of people to share this incredible journey with.

After I finished breakfast, I went to the lobby and sat in the darkened room while the rest of group was still eating. I was still enveloped in the darkness when I spotted a familiar face across the room sitting on the couch. It was Cimela. She and her filmmaking partner Sean had arrived the night before.

Cimela got up and spotted me and came over and gave me a hug. The *light* this woman carries within her soul, helped the darkness leave. My soul picked up on that quickly. That was definitely a grace from Our Lord. We chatted a bit before we all headed to Mass. By the time morning Mass had ended, the *feeling* of darkness was completely gone. It was as though it was never there in the first place. I felt exhausted though. Having received Our Lord ever present in the Holy Eucharist, I was ready for the day.

We had an opportunity as part of our pilgrimage, to have a question and answer session with Mirjana in her pansion. There were only around thirty of us there and so we had more than the typical amount of time with her. They say that usually the dining area where this takes place is packed with pilgrims and that the Q and A sessions aren't as long as we had that day. The weather was even way better than it was forecasted for our stay. We were incredibly blessed with things like this throughout our trip! Thank you Lord!

I had prepared some questions that I had saved on my phone to ask Mirjana after I read her book but it didn't seem like good questions by the time we got started. A question did come to me though. I asked her what she thought about people, especially online social media reports like I wrote about earlier in this chapter, being so anti-Medjugorje. I said that these came from some so-called orthodox Catholics. Mirjana responded in Croatian and Miki Musa interpreted her response. Mirjana speaks English, but it's easier for her in this format. She said, "they're not Catholic then". She explained that we as Catholics shouldn't criticize or say such negative things about fellow Catholics. If someone says to her that they also "see" the Holy Virgin, she said she first would check it out herself but would be supportive and not criticize. That's what we as Catholics should do, be supportive and not tear down. I then said to her about the doubts I had especially when I would read these "reports" against her and Medjugorje. I told her that after I had read her book, and reading her account about the apparitions and the severe persecution that she faced early on, it erased every doubt I had. I told her that her words convinced me. She said many books have been written about her and the apparitions and they never even once approached her about it. These people created many false stories.

She was so sweet and kind to us. She's the *real deal* as they say. She posed for pictures with us and signed our books as well. Some of the group afterwards, told me that I asked a very good question. Sean Bloomfield, who helped Mirjana on her book, told me that Mirjana really appreciated what I said about her book. It was a great experience hearing from a visionary. I honestly can say it was like having a Q&A session with St Bernadette of Lourdes or the Fatima seers.

The group also had the opportunity to climb Mt. Krizevac or as its known to many, Cross Mountain. Cross Mountain is known for its massive twenty-five foot high cross over looking Medjugorje. Construction of the cross began in 1933 to commentate the 1900th anniversary of Our Lord Jesus' passion and death. The Holy Father, Pius XI, proclaimed 1933 has a jubilee year of the Cross. A relic of the *True Cross* of Our Lord is contained within it. Huge Stations of the Cross plaques are set up all the way up Cross Mountain. It's much more of a climb than Apparition Hill.

Miki our guide led our group in praying the Stations as we climbed up this very steep and rocky mountain. We were given plenty of time to pray as we reached the top of the mountain. A couple of pilgrims from our group saw the sun *moving* while we were at the top. The *Miracle of the Sun* which became famous in Fatima, Portugal on October 13, 1917, during Our Lady's Apparition there, is often *experienced* by pilgrims in Medjugorje. I myself didn't see it. It's *shown* to those who it's meant to be for. What an incredible blessing for them!

From the other pilgrimage group, an Eastern Catholic priest, Father Christopher Crotty came along with them. The Eastern Catholic rite is in full communion with Rome. Father Crotty is very passionate and is well educated in the faith. He gave incredible lessons in the Catholic Faith after our days were done. Most of the group gathered as Father Crotty went into some intense teachings. Some even took notes and recorded his talks with their phones. We asked him plenty of questions about the Catholic Faith and he answered them with such great depth. It was fascinating to say the least.

Father Crotty is well known for his healing ministry. I believe he spent around eighteen-years in this ministry. He's now as of this writing living a monastic life. He did although, give many in our group a healing service in the small chapel of the Two Hearts pansion. Our group was moved to the Two Hearts from Mirjana's pansion to make way for a large group of Italian pilgrims coming in. The Italians are probably the biggest group of pilgrims who comes on pilgrimage to Medjugorje since it's just across the Adriatic Sea.

When our healing service began, Father Crotty first explained to us about healing. There are three forms of healing he said, the spiritual, physical and moral healing. He then did some Eastern Catholic chants and their forms of prayer, which is prayed in quick succession. We then repeated some of the responses in chant. He then blessed us all with some anointing oil. I don't remember the specific name of it but it had a beautiful aroma. He then had us line up side by side for those of us who didn't have a chair in this small chapel. He proceeded to *lay hands* on us. Many fell because they were *resting in the spirit*. It's more commonly known as *slain in the spirit* but Father Crotty doesn't like to refer to it as that. He said it sounded violent for the Holy Spirit to *slain* someone.

I was next to Cimela when Father got to me. I didn't *rest* as most others had; I didn't *feel* anything until he moved on. I knelt and then that's when I *received* a powerful vision.

I heard Our Lord say to me, "don't you trust Me?" a couple of times. He was wearing a white robe with a red sash and I said, "I do Lord". I believe that it was in reference to one of the reasons of my coming to Medjugorje, to be healed of the Type 1 Diabetes. I've been praying so much for it that I eventually strayed in trusting Him in knowing that He's heard my petitions and will answer them. He then *showed* me a very large crowd of people off to my right side. He just stretched out His arm pointing to them. Our Lord didn't say anything but I *understood* what I was being *shown*. The Lord was *showing* me all the people who I was going to encounter in the future who I was going to pray over. It was to pray for healing to be exact. This powerful vision came with the pain and suffering of all these souls. It made me cry because it was overwhelming. The tears just started just like that.

The pain of these souls gave way to this great peace. What an incredible vision! I know that there's work to be done in terms of being used as instrument of the Lord's healing. As poor of an instrument as I am, the Lord's Mercy will still triumph.

Father Crotty said the effects of the healing prayers, are gradual. He said we all must continue to pray to the Holy Spirit to complete our healings.

I was able to speak to Father Crotty alone a few days before this service about healing, in regards to what I *received* as wrote about earlier in this book. His response was to let the Holy Spirit work. Allowing the Spirit to work will open me up to more Charisms needed for my own ministry. His message, and the one message that was prevalent during this pilgrimage was, have an open heart. Complete openness to Our Lord, and to the Queen of Peace will allow miracles to take place. One of the biggest healings taken place in

Medjugorje is the one of the heart. There are plenty of miraculous physical healings that take place here but it's the one of the interior that matters most.

March 18th, the day of Mirjana's yearly apparition finally arrived. From her previous messages, we will know in time why March 18th was chosen for these particular apparitions.

Our morning of the 18th started out with breakfast and then we immediately proceeded to the spot of the apparitions. It has been taken place at the Blue Cross at the base of Apparition Hill for some time now. The Blue Cross is where Our Lady once appeared to one of the visionaries in the early years and a cross was put up to mark the spot.

Rain was forecasted for that day and the thought was that the apparition was going to take place inside Mirjana's pansion. The weather miraculously cleared up for us this day and other days when rain was certain. Rain was not a factor despite it being forecasted for the majority of our trip. Thank you Lord!

The group got to the Blue Cross around 9am. The apparition usually takes place around 2pm. We got there early because an influx of pilgrims was expected. We were able to get an incredibly close vantage point to Mirjana. Our little group started a Rosary after an Italian group finished praying theirs in Italian. Just a short time later a small band came along and played some songs before the scheduled official Rosaries were to begin. At this point, to me, this experience became otherworldly. The recitation of the Rosary by all of us pilgrims, as the crowd began to fill in as expected, was amazing. The band also played like a Charismatic version of *Kumbaya* and *Immaculate Mary* and another song I didn't recognize in Croatian, Italian and English in between the Mysteries. The atmosphere was electric. We recited about four Rosaries by the time some cheers broke out in the distance as Mirjana began making her way towards the apparition spot. This was about 1:30pm or so.

Some of our group and myself were just behind the Blue Cross and the statue of Our Lady, which is there as well. We were up and to the left if you are facing the front of the cross. Film crews were set up right in front of us on both sides of the cross. Cimela was set up there as well with her video equipment.

We finally see Mirjana emerge through the crowd with Sean Bloomfield guiding her by hand. The area around the Blue Cross has some stone pews, which were occupied by special guests of Mirjana I assume. There were many priests in this roped off area as well, including Father Crotty.

The first thing I was given to *feel* and *sense* prior to Mirjana's arrival was the strong presence of the Holy Angels. I could *see* them encircling the base of Apparition Hill as though they were checking out the area. The Angels were huge with long flowing robes. I *felt* their presence many times before in the past but they seemed larger than usual this day.

Mirjana greeted all the priests before she knelt down on the rocky floor right in front of the Cross. She then joined in the recitation of the Rosary. Sean knelt right next to her on her left side. Many people were recording these very anxious and exciting moments with their cell phones including myself. Several minutes passed and Mirjana began to rock back and forth almost shivering it seemed like, which I was told was unusual. As I had my phone lifted up recording at this point, I was trying to be in the moment, meaning keeping myself in prayer. Then all of sudden, the actual feeling of being lifted off the ground hit me. It was as though I was beginning to float. I had to look down to honestly see if I was. I was not. This caught me off guard. It was a couple of minutes after that, that Our Lady appeared to Mirjana. Her back and forth and jittery motion gave way to a gasp and a look to the sky with an enormous smile on her face. I could see that she was conversing with Our Lady. I then began to *hear* the conversation but I couldn't understand the language. It seemed as though I wasn't supposed to *hear* what was being said because I had the *understanding* that it wasn't for me. It was somewhat muffled as well. I then turned my focus on Mirjana. If I wasn't supposed to *listen* in, then I wanted to see if I was able to *feel* what she was feeling. This may have been the first time perhaps, that this *Empathic Gift* from the Holy Spirit, was used in this way. I don't remember if I purposefully ever tried to *feel* a certain person's emotions on cue. Whatever the case, the Spirit of the Lord allowed me to *feel* Mirjana at that moment.

I *felt* her joy, but not at her level because again, the apparition was not meant for me per se. I did *feel* her pain at a high level though right before Our Lady left. When this hurt came to me, it was just moments before Mirjana visibly changed in her demeanor as the apparition ended. I *knew* the apparition was about to end because of what I *felt*. These feelings didn't linger because like for most people there, this incredible experience was mesmerizing to all present. We all saw how drained Mirjana looked at this point as she almost collapsed. Some of the group commented later on how they felt sympathy for her. To see the whole apparition first hand and to see what she goes through, and what she's gone through over the last thirty-eight years, one can't help but have sympathy for her. She's a very special soul.

Our Lady's message was then dictated to Miki and to another woman as well. The message was then roughly translated and given to the crowd in Croatian, English and then Italian. The final and proper translation was released just hours later. The message given was:

"Dear children,

My earthly life was simple. I loved and I rejoiced in small things. I loved life – the gift from God – even though pain and sufferings pierced my heart.

My children, I had the strength of faith and boundless trust in God's love. All those who have the strength of faith are stronger. Faith makes you live according to what is good and then the light of God's love always comes at the desired moment. That is the strength, which sustains in pain and suffering.

My children, pray for the strength of faith, trust in the Heavenly Father, and do not be afraid. Know that not a single creature who belongs to God will be lost but will live forever. Every pain has its end and then life in freedom begins there where all of my children come – where everything is returned.

My children, your battle is difficult. It will be even more difficult, but you follow my example. Pray for the strength of faith; trust in the love of the Heavenly Father.

I am with you. I am manifesting myself to you. I am encouraging you. With immeasurable motherly love I am caressing your souls. Thank you."

What a beautiful message from the Queen of Peace. This pilgrimage definitely made a tremendous impact on me. The call from Our Lady for me was to go deeper into prayer, to meditate deeper during the Holy Rosary and to continue to pray for souls, in particular healing. The group also played a big part in the incredible spiritual journey I was on in Medjugorje. Each one of us were called by Our Lady individually to come here, but we were called to experience this beautiful pilgrimage together.

Queen of Peace, pray for us!

Chapter 2: The Call

After the events of my 2018 pilgrimage to Medjugorje these *interior locutions* from Our Lady increased. As I described in my last book, my prayer life became more focused and more spiritual. I was already praying in an extensive way before Medjugorje but what occurred there and what I learned from there, helped advance my prayer life. It's only by the Holy Spirit that this occurred. Like I've written many times before, it's nothing of my doing.

After our Rosary Group learned of the *locutions*, these visions of Our Lady became a regular occurrence. It wasn't just limited to the Rosary anymore. It started to occur when I would pray alone in my bedroom. I would invoke Our Lady and She would come. These *intellectual visions* as they are called, were some very powerful experiences for me. It was and still is an incredible grace.

The intensity really picked up in June of 2018 as we were praying our weekly Rosary in the Prayer Garden.

I received a powerful vision after the First Glorious Mystery as we gathered on this Sunday. The vision began as it felt as though I was literally transported to Apparition Hill back in Medjugorje. I could see the white colored rocks as it felt I was slightly floating above the very rocky and jagged terrain. I saw everything so clearly. I then saw Mirjana Soldo very clearly. She was kneeling like she does during the apparitions at the Blue

Cross during the 2nd of every month. I then was given to *see* how she sees Our Lady during these Heavenly visions and then I saw how Our Lady viewed Mirjana and the rest of the pilgrims there. I could see all the pilgrims down below at that point, as I was way above Apparition Hill looking down. I didn't know why I *received* all this at this point but my heart wanted to explode with joy with all the feelings I felt during this vision. The vision ended and I was back in the Prayer Garden with a ton of questions. Why was I shown Medjugorje and Mirjana during this vision? I got my answer about ten days later during another vision from Our Lady.

This vision took place in my bedroom. I invoked Our Lady and Her brief message to me when I asked the meaning of the vision from the Prayer Garden was, "I have work for you to do there". I obviously assumed it was to take place in Medjugorje because of the vision from Sunday.

Then during the Rosary of June 27, in the Prayer Garden in the heat of our Texas Summers, Our Lady said the *work* was "to transmit messages to those who are seeking Her." I was to be an instrument in that. "So many come to here (Medjugorje) for healing as well," Our Lady said to me. I will be used for that purpose in addition to that. It's just not for the physical healing but for the healing of the heart as well. Our Lady said that She wished to heal everyone who comes to Medjugorje. I was also to relay this *work* to Mirjana. This understanding that was infused, seemed to me like it would take thirty days for the *work* to be accomplished. My time in Medjugorje Our Lady said was to coincide with Cimela Kidonakis. This meant my way to get there would be through Stella Mar Pilgrimages once again. They were the team I went with in March of 2018. Our Lady also said that *they* (a priest or someone else?) would know I was sent by Her. Our Lady continued saying that She would provide the ways and means to get to Medjugorje and complete Her *work*. I saw many people on Apparition Hill during this particular vision of *the call*. I believe it was the same people that the Lord showed me during the vision at the healing service that Father Crotty performed for us that I wrote about in the previous chapter.

Our Lady's message to Mirjana Soldo on July 2, 2018 added a new twist so to speak to this *call* and *work* that I was called to.

July 02, 2018

"Dear children, I am the mother of all of you and, therefore, do not be afraid because I hear your prayers. I know that you seek me and that is why I am praying to my Son for you, my Son, who is united with the Heavenly Father and the Holy Spirit - the Paraclete - my Son who leads souls to the Kingdom from where He came, the Kingdom of peace and light. My children, you are given the freedom to choose, but, as a mother, I implore you to choose the freedom for the good. You, with pure and simple souls comprehend - even if sometimes you do not understand the words - and within yourselves you feel what the truth is. My children, do not lose the truth and true life so as to follow the false one. By life in truth, the Kingdom of Heaven enters into your hearts, and that is the Kingdom of peace, love and harmony. Then, my children, there will not be the selfishness which

distances you from my Son. There will be love and understanding for your neighbors. Because, remember, again I repeat to you, to pray also means to love others, your neighbors, and to give yourself to them. Love and give in my Son, and then He will work in you and for you. My children, ceaselessly think of my Son and love Him immeasurably and you will have true life, and that will be for eternity. Thank you, apostles of my love."

Chapter 3: The Messages

As I've written before about the monthly messages of Our Lady in Medjugorje, they have been a mainstay since the beginning. These messages to the World given to Mirjana and Marija are once a month on the 2nd and 25th respectively. It is in these monthly messages that Our Lady granted me another connection to Medjugorje.

When I read Our Lady's message to Mirjana on July 2nd, I was ecstatic because the first part of that message, was what Our Lady had told me during the vision a week earlier. It was as though She used the first part of that message to confirm to me what She had told me about the *work* that She wanted me to do. I was over the moon about this but also a little perplexed on why Our Lady used this message to Mirjana to confirm to me the vision from June.

Our weekly Rosaries continued every Sunday and Our Lady began to further show me what She wanted me to do in Medjugorje. I would also *receive* these incredible instructions during my personal prayer time at my home as well. Invoking Our Lady during this time at home was as powerful as it was during our Parish Rosaries. I began at this point writing down everything that occurred during these *visits* from Our Lady.

By the middle of July I began to make plans to travel to Medjugorje to do Our Lady's *work*. I told my mother first on what Our Lady was calling me to do. She had a somewhat surprised look on her face. With my father and her being a part of the Charismatic Renewal Movement for many years, this wasn't a total shock for her. My parents would travel all over the Dallas/Ft. Worth area and sometimes way beyond, by the prompting of the Holy Spirit, to do the Lord's work as part of this Movement. It has been many years since they've done this type of *work* though. Health issues and age have contributed to this being so.

My next step was to seek travel arrangements. Our Lady had said that my time there would coincide with Cimela Kidonakis and so it was clear as I stated before that I was to use Stella Mar Pilgrimages once again since Cimela is a partner this pilgrimage company. The Blessed Mother through all these interior locutions said that She would provide the means and ways for me to get there. So obviously per my nature I tried to force things along which didn't work too well.

The first opening with Stella Mar was in the early Fall of 2018 and that pilgrimage was all booked. The next one was to be a New Year's pilgrimage but that was canceled for lack of interest for that time of the year. It was at this point that I realized that I had to step way, way back and let Our Lady do it Her way. Lo and behold, things started to work out in a miraculous way in order for me to travel to Medjugorje once again.

The monthly messages from Our Lady to Mirjana started to have a familiar ring to them. When August 2nd's message came out to the World, I looked back on my notes and I saw once again that I had already received some of the message beforehand during the inner locutions I received from Our Lady. Then it happened again with September's message. When it happened a third time in a row, I began to understand that a connection to Medjugorje had been established.

As the 2nd of October was approaching, I was anxiously waiting to see if Our Lady's message to Mirjana would be something I had already received either during our weekly Parish Rosary or during the visions I received during the week. When the message came out I quickly went through my notes on my phone to see if it a match and sure enough it was.

The matches would at times be some parts of the message or at times be a large part of it. The part of this incredible connection that there was no denying it was a match is what I received was verbatim to what was relayed to the World from Medjugorje.

There were times I would give testimony inspired by the Holy Spirit either to the Rosary Group or to my Confirmation Class or even to certain individuals, and what I would say to them, would also be what Our Lady passed along to Mirjana on later date. I would even comment to the Rosary Group that what I spoke about, gave testimony about, on a previous occasion to them, was passed along to the World on a later date from Medjugorje. This happened multiple times.

There would be occasions during the Rosary or during my own private prayer time, that I would be *shown* Mirjana at the Blue Cross in Medjugorje as she is during the monthly Apparitions. These visions were so clear. I *knew* that when I *saw* Mirjana, it was typically a sign that what I was about to *receive* at that moment would be what the World would receive at a future Apparition in Medjugorje from Our Lady. These were powerful visions when this occurred. It was as though I was physically present in Medjugorje during these monthly Apparitions.

October also marked my *connection* to a second visionary from Medjugorje, Marija Pavlovic-Lunetti. During a vision at my home, I *saw* Marija. I *knew* that what I *received* that particular night was a future message to the World from Our Lady to Marija. When the 25th of October came and Marija *received* her message from Our Lady to World, it was something I had already *received* from the Blessed Mother. Marija's messages come on the 25th of every month from Our Lady as I've stated before.

I was now *receiving* advanced messages from Our Lady that was given to two Medjugorje visionaries. When I would ask Our Lady why, She would say that it was to establish that there was a *connection* between Medjugorje and myself.

On one occasion during a vision from Our Lady, She said to me that what I had *received* was a rare grace. This Heavenly grace to *communicate* with the Queen of Heaven.

These advanced messages continued the rest of 2018 and into 2019. There was a lot more that Our Lady would pass along to me in terms of *communications* but that was either some personal things for me or something personal that needed to be passed along to someone in which I did shortly after my March 2018 pilgrimage to Medjugorje. That message was received by the recipient with a very neutral response. They neither rebuked it nor accepted it. This recipient was a fellow pilgrim from that trip. I'm not 100% sure why this person didn't accept this message to be authentic since they've been to Medjugorje numerous times and are familiar with God's wonders there through Our Lady. I did my part in delivering the message. It's not my job to convince them to believe it. It is a little difficult not to take it personal though.

There is a third visionary, Jakov Colo who receives a yearly Apparition from Our Lady on Christmas Day. I was very interested in seeing if that day's message to the World from Our Lady was something I had already *received*. It wasn't. I wasn't too surprised by that.

The details of the *work* became more specific during these many visions I *received* in the second half of 2018 and in early 2019. Many times I *saw* people praying on Apparition Hill during these supernatural encounters with Our Lady. It was confirmed by the Blessed Mother that the people I *saw* during the vision at the Healing Service performed by Father Crotty that I wrote about in Chapter 1, were the people I was to encounter on my future pilgrimage to Medjugorje. These were the people I was going to pray for and to also pass along Our Lady messages to them.

Our Lady said I was to approach a person who was pointed out to me and I was to say to them "Our Lady wants me to pray with you". It was during this time that I would *receive* whatever it was that Our Lady had for them. She also said that this *work* would be very exhausting and very draining on me. She also said that the *evil one* would try to disrupt me as well. I knew that part of the reason that the pilgrimage was later rather than sooner like I wanted, was because I needed to be ready for what was needed to be done there. Looking back, I clearly needed a lot of preparation spiritually to be able to accomplish this *mission*. Our Lord and Our Lady clearly worked on my soul during these long months heading into 2019. Our Lady had also instructed me to relay everything to Mirjana Soldo. I know from my previous pilgrimage that this was a tall task especially since Mirjana hosts many pilgrims and to have time to speak to her at length is not an easy thing. The other thing Our Lady instructed was that a particular pilgrim who was to be on this long stay of mine, was to chronicle the *work*. I'm not sure in which way that this was to be done. I asked Our Lady many times on how this would work since this pilgrim was surely to be busy during the pilgrimage itself. Our Lady said that this pilgrim "had a choice to serve". She said that they have free will to choose if they wanted to chronicle or not and if they said that they were too busy, I was to say to them "if you want to serve Our Lady you will find the time". This seemed like another tall task. I struggled a lot with this last instruction, as this particular pilgrim was the same pilgrim I gave the message from Our Lady after my first trip to Medjugorje. I know I needed to do a lot of praying on these tasks from the Queen of Heaven.

By November of 2018 I was able to book my pilgrimage to Medjugorje for late February of 2019. I was to leave February 27th and come back on March 20, 2019. It wasn't quite the thirty days I had thought it to be but three weeks is what Our Lady wanted. I was excited to say the least.

I went on a pilgrimage to Eastern Europe in November of 2018 with my parents and my sister Maria which was an incredible blessing as well. We visited Krakow, Poland as part of the pilgrimage. The blessing to see the resting place of St. Faustina once again was an incredible grace. I had been to Poland once before during World Youth Day 2016. To revisit some of the places I visited back in 2016 was amazing. The one place I visited once again on this pilgrimage was the Auschwitz Death Camp. The tour we took on this trip was different from my first trip there in 2016. I didn't *feel* what I did back in 2016, which I wrote about in my first book *My Life in the Supernatural: A Story of Divine Mercy*. I believe the Lord shielded me in a way this time around and also I didn't really want to focus on *feeling* everything there like I did on my first trip there. I did *feel* some heaviness and sadness in the beginning of this particular tour but mostly I felt horrified and saddened at the capacity of human evilness that occurred there so many years ago. The stark reminders left there in Auschwitz are truly heartbreaking.

One of the signs of God's Divine Providence for this particular pilgrimage to Eastern Europe was to formally meet a fellow pilgrim from our group who had been on previous pilgrimages with me and my family that I've been on since 2008. Pamela Cooper was truly a Godsend. Pam was very instrumental in answering a lot of my questions involving the supernatural occurrences that the Lord and Our Lady had granted me. Pam has *received* many supernatural experiences herself and she was able to offer her inspired take on many things on what I had *received*. She became a trusted friend and was very helpful in the months leading up to my pilgrimage to Medjugorje coming up in February 2019. The Lord granted her many things to aid me in this journey to this small village in Bosnia-Herzegovina.

A dream I had in August of 2018 also played a big part of my *work* that was to take place in Medjugorje.

Chapter 4: Meghan

In August of 2018 I had a dream that was very profound to me at the time and little did I know how profound the dream ended up being.

In this dream, I seemed to be in Medjugorje but I did not recognize the exact place I was at. At first I was in what seemed like a back area or a concourse of a sports arena or large auditorium. I see a line of priest processing from this area towards an entrance of the arena. They were all dressed in their albs and stoles. One of the priests had Our Lord, ever present in the Holy Eucharist, in a large golden monstrance. He stops in front of me and I kneel before Our Lord in reverence. I then make my way in the arena/auditorium and I see people in the stands. I see this brilliant light shining upon this small section of people as I'm facing them with my back towards this brilliant light. I immediately sense that it's Our Lady who is in this light. I recognize that I'm there to do the *work*, to communicate Her messages to the faithful, individually. I then see that my friend from my first pilgrimage to Medjugorje Erin Pynes is assisting me. Then I see the first person that I was called upon to pray for. This woman with long brown hair and glasses is seated on the bottom row of this section of seats that I'm facing. There was some railing separating this small group from me. The bottom row was slightly elevated from where I was standing. I was like in the walking area of this section but I was close enough to the bottom row of people to pray over them one by one.

The woman with the brown hair, which was a little curly, appeared to be in her 50s. I'm very bad in guessing ages but she did appear somewhat older than I was as I'm in my mid-40s. I could see this brilliant light on this woman's face very clearly. It was because of this light, that this woman's face was seared into my memory after I had awakened from this incredible dream. There was a small time jump at this point because the next thing I remember was that I had just prayed over this woman and I had given her a message from Our Lady. She was crying as the tears from her face glistened from the brilliant light from Our Lady. Her face appeared somewhat saddened from whatever it was I had just told her. I felt absolutely drained at this point. I was able to recall what Our Lady had said to me about how this *work* was going to be draining. I then took a deep breath and I went to the next person seated to the left of the woman whom I had just passed on a Heavenly message from the Mother of God. Erin moved right along with me as I got the next person. Erin appeared to be carrying some sort of writing pad. This also fit to what Our Lady had said about the *work* being chronicled. It was at this point that I woke up with the beautiful peace knowing that Our Lady had given me glimpse of what She wanted from me in terms of the *work* in Medjugorje. This dream was confirmation for me on all that I had *received* from Our Lady.

The one other detail about this dream was that the whole arena/auditorium seemed to have the lights dimmed way down. This made this brilliant light from Our Lady even more pronounced on the people on this particular section.

I relayed this dream to one of my nephews shortly after

this and he asked if I would remember the woman from my dream if I were ever to encounter her in real life in the future. I said, "yes I would." This dream was that profound to me at the time.

As I wrote about in my first book in the chapter about dreams, the Lord had granted me these incredible prophetic dreams on a regular occurrence. Part of these *future* dreams were encounters with people in my dreams whom I would encounter in the future in real life. Many a times these people were complete strangers to me. I would journal a lot of these dreams in the first years of my journey. It was amazing to match up the details from my dream to these real life encounters with these people.

On October 2nd during my viewing of Stella Mar's footage of Mirjana's monthly Apparition, there was a young woman kneeling to the right of Mirjana who got my attention. This beautiful blonde woman with her shortened hair brushed back was tearfully praying next to Mirjana. In the days leading up to the Apparition on one of Stella Mar's social media pages, this young woman was featured in some of their online posts. In these pictures, this young woman was sitting with some of Stella Mar's other pilgrims enjoying dinner at one of the restaurants that line the streets across St. James Church.

Mirjana's message from Our Lady on October 2nd became the fourth month in a row that I had received some part of that message beforehand.

Stella Mar put out another video just shortly after the Apparition of October 2nd. The video featured the same stylish young blonde woman who was next to Mirjana. This was woman Meghan Schexnayder-Greco.

Meghan who was on her first pilgrimage to Medjugorje was a Louisiana native. Her mother and father had been on a pilgrimage to Medjugorje with Stella Mar the year before in 2017. This was their first pilgrimage to Medjugorje together. During her video testimony, Meghan testified how she was diagnosed with bone cancer seven years prior. She had some surgeries to place titanium rods in one of her arms and one of legs. After many treatments over the years, the doctors gave her a dire prognosis in the beginning of 2018. They said that she only had 6-12 months to live. During the past year and a half or so, Meghan said that her spiritual journey took on a serious turn. She was able to reconcile herself to the Lord prior to her pilgrimage to Medjugorje. Meghan said that she did ask Our Lady for healing during Mirjana's Apparition but she was asking more so for all the others who were out there that day asking for their own blessings.

After this beautiful and heartbreaking testimony, I went back to the posts that Stella Mar had prior to the Apparition and I see that several women were tagged in these online photos. One name was Angie Schexnayder. I figured she was somehow related to Meghan. I was able to find that Angie had her own social media page. My heart raced as I came to the stunning realization that Angie was the woman from my dream from August. There was absolutely no doubt in mind. Angie, I came to find out was Meghan's mother.

Why the dream? What's the connection? These

questions and more raced through my mind as I tried to unravel this supernatural mystery. It was near my bedtime and so I had to get on my knees to pray as it felt as though I was on the precipice of a panic attack. I was able to sleep some by God's grace that night.

I believe it was the next day or so that I contacted my pilgrimage group from March of 2018 via a group chat on a message app on my phone. I recounted to the group all that had transpired with the messages from Medjugorje, the visions, the locutions, and the dream of Meghan's mother Angie. I had to tell someone, as this revelation of the dream connection became a little too much for me to handle.

I was given some advice and some support from everyone in the group on these matters which was such a relief. I thank Our Lady for bringing us together. I felt relief that someone outside my family and Rosary group knew what was happening with what Our Lord and Our Lady had given me concerning Medjugorje.

After a lot of prayer, I was given to discern that the purpose of the dream of Angie was to relay a message.

At first though, my initial reaction was perhaps that I needed to go to Louisiana pray and over Meghan as Our Lady had given me to *know* that part of my *work* was to pray over people for healing. So naturally I thought that this was my *mission* concerning Meghan.

It was not too long that Our Lady had given me through Her *communications*, that a message was needed to be passed along but it wasn't to be right away. Events had to unfold first, namely the untimely passing of Meghan.

There was a second dream I had in October that further confirmed what I was given by Our Lady about Meghan and her family to be true.

In this dream, I'm walking in Medjugorje in front of St. James Church. The area in front of the Church was different though. The Church was siting in a neighborhood that one typically sees in a small town anywhere in United States. The small quaint houses sitting side by side was in stark contrast to the famous two bell towers of St. James that could be seen above the tree lines from miles away. As I'm walking along the sidewalk in front of St. James, I see a priest sitting in a chair with another man sitting right in front of him on the grass area in front of the bell tower furthest from me. As I got closer, I see that this priest is hearing the confession of this man sitting in front of him. I make my way off the sidewalk and I started walking on the street as I pass them by so as not to hear the confession.

I take look at this priest who was hearing the confession as I passed by. He was of an African descent as I picked up his African accent as he was speaking English to the penitent man sitting across from him. It was at this point that I woke up.

A couple of days later I saw a video that was posted by Meghan's family on a social media page about their pilgrimage to Medjugorje. The video was a testimony about their trip. Meghan was featured of course but then a priest who was part of the same pilgrimage begins his testimony about the trip. Once again my heart jumped as I recognized this priest from my dream a couple of days earlier. This priest was Father Anthony Odiong who is of a Nigerian descent. As he spoke in this video it was the same African accent I heard from my dream. From what I gathered through the video testimony and from some social media posts about him from the Schexnayder family, he is very close to them. So it made sense that I was given to *see* him in my dream.

Our Lady was just granting me more confirmation and the courage to carry out what She wanted me to do, and that was to be Her voice to them about Meghan.

One of the things that Meghan said in the video, which was further confirmation of the *work*, was "put your words in me and I will be your vessel." This is what Our Lady was calling for me to do in regards to passing along Her messages.

I prepared a long message explaining everything to Angie as I was given to discern that this was the way I was to be Her "voice", as Our Lady put it. This particular pilgrimage that the Schexnayder's were on in October to Medjugorje, was one of the pilgrimages I wanted to go on but it was completely booked. I often think what would've happened had I'd been there on that particular pilgrimage. It just wasn't part of God's plan for me to be there.

I was still *seeing* Meghan during the many visions of Our Lady heading towards the end of 2018. I would ask Our Lady why I kept *seeing* Meghan during these visions. It was all in preparation for the *message* for her mother Angie. It was also so I could pray for them as well.

The Blessed Mother had given me to know that

Meghan's "time is short" as She relayed this message to me. Her words were truly prophetic as Meghan passed away on January 15, 2019. Meghan had gotten married just a month earlier in December of 2018. I was heartbroken when I heard of her passing. This was someone whom I had never met but yet it felt as though I had known her for years because of Our Lady.

By the end of January of 2019, Our Lady had given me to *know* that the time had come to deliver Her *words* to Angie. I then proceeded to do so. For obvious reasons, I will not disclose what Our Lady had to say to her, as it was personal.

I didn't get a reply back from Angie but Our Lady did give me to *know* what will come from the *message* in time.

I struggled mightily in sending this *message* to Meghan's mother but I knew that this was what She was calling me to do in Medjugorje. That constant thought gave me the courage to send it.

A message of this nature might sound impersonal to the reader but this is what was called for from Our Lady. I trust in that. Like I stated before, what I was "given" by Our Lady regarding the future of this particular matter, will makes sense of why the *message* was delivered the way it was.

This was a very powerful and delicate way to begin this *work* of Our Lady as February 27th the day of my departure to Medjugorje was quickly approaching.

I will end this chapter with Our Lady's message to

Mirjana Soldo from October 2, 2018 in which Meghan was present kneeling next to Mirjana during the apparition.

"Dear children, I am calling you to be courageous and to not grow weary, because even the smallest good - the smallest sign of love - conquers evil which is all the more visible. My children, listen to me so that good may overcome, so that you may come to know the love of my Son. This is the greatest happiness - the hands of my Son that embrace, of Him who loves the soul, of Him who has given Himself for you and is always giving Himself anew in the Eucharist, of Him who has the words of eternal life. To come to know His love, to follow in His footsteps, means to have a wealth of spirituality. This is the wealth, which gives good feelings and sees love and goodness everywhere. Apostles of my love, my children, be like the rays of the sun, which with the warmth of my Son's love warm everyone around them. My children, the world needs apostles of love; the world needs much prayer, but prayer spoken with the heart and the soul and not only pronounced with the lips. My children, long for holiness but in humility, in the humility which permits my Son to do that which He desires through you. My children, your prayers, your words, thoughts and actions - all of this either opens or closes the doors to the Kingdom of Heaven for you. My Son showed you the way and gave you hope, and I am consoling and encouraging you because, my children, I had come to know pain, but I had faith and hope. Now I have the reward of life in the Kingdom of my Son. Therefore, listen to me, have courage and do not grow weary. Thank you."

Chapter 5: Pre-Medjugorje 2019

Leading up to my departure date to Medjugorje on February 27, 2019, there were some very powerful visions that took place. The biggest one was a vision of Hell. This was the second time that I had received such a vision. The first one was at the beginning months of my conversion in 2006 in which I wrote about in my first book.

This dark vision took place on January 19, 2019, in my bedroom as I prayed calling upon Our Lady. As the Blessed Mother appeared, She said that She wanted to take me on a journey this night. At first it felt as though it was all me saying these words to myself but as I continued praying and as I further gathered myself, it was truly the words of Our Lady as She repeated those same words "I wish to take you on a journey", and at once I was taken to a place of fire. She said, "This is a place where souls come who are lost and are in total despair. These are souls who separated themselves from My Son." It was at that point I saw a huge lake of fire and I saw souls falling in and then coming out as blackened figures. I felt great fear as I could *feel* it all. My whole body felt it. I sensed great evil as it was still lingering with me as I wrote an account of it shortly after the vision had ended and I had come to grips of what I was *shown* this night. Our Lady had also said "My Son has given you a great grace in praying for souls (praying for mercy for them before their deaths) that were heading there (Hell) if not for this (particular) grace. My Son wishes for you to continue praying for souls as such as many have been saved. Pray unceasingly for these souls (as I've been given to *see* and pray for)." She also said that this is what She showed *Her Children*. I'm assuming the Medjugorje visionaries. I believe two of the six visionaries had been given to *see* Hell. Our Lady said that what I was given to *see* and *experience*, was only a small glimpse of Hell. She then said that She will be guiding me in bringing souls to Her Son. Our Lady had a real urgency and seriousness to Her tone that night. This vision had drained me. I trust that this vision was another *connection* to Medjugorje.

Our Lady had forewarned me that the evil one would be out in full force to discourage me leading up to pilgrimage. In a dream I had shortly before this vision of Hell proved that.

The dream began with me being with Mirjana during an Apparition in Medjugorje. I was next to her as a large crowd surrounded us. The Apparition site seemed to take place in an enclosed area that I didn't recognize. I was able to hold Mirjana's hand as we began praying. It was about a second before Our Lady came that I sensed a rush of emotion swell within me at a rapid pace. I then said, "She's coming!" This was right before Mirjana *saw* Our Lady. We both then physically reacted. I couldn't *see* the Blessed Mother like Mirjana did at that moment and that seemed somewhat strange to me. I then began to have vision of random things that I don't really remember what they were. The only image from the vision that I do remember was that of Ronald Reagan. I then *heard* many voices but not that of Our Lady. I then said out loud "this is not of God!" in a somewhat frightened tone. At that moment the evilness behind this false apparition became exposed as I sensed its evil presence. At that moment, Mirjana and I had another visible reaction as before but this time it wasn't the Heavenly rush but that of an evil one. I believe Mirjana began to scream writhing in agony or fright while some people rushed to her. I seemed to have fallen back almost being back in my bedroom in bed as I saw these evil shadows being projected on the ceiling. I tried swiping them away with little avail. I woke up at that instant with the deep presence of evil still around me. It was very strong. I got up and sprinkled holy water all around my room. This evil presence and dream drained me. I believe the evil one was trying to discourage me like Our Lady had said.

Another powerful vision also took place in January that's worth noting. In this vision Our Lady came with a feeling of sadness. She appeared as Our Lady of Grace. The sadness was because of the New York Abortion Law that had passed allowing abortions up until birth and the bombing of a Catholic Church in the Philippines that killed twenty plus souls and injured scores more. That bombing was the *feeling* that I had *received* the day before when I was waiting to go to Confession. This *death feeling* was also with me later that same night. I was able to pray a Chaplet of Divine Mercy for these precious souls who lost their lives in this horrendous terrorist act.

Our Lady said in this particular vision that "We must pray and make reparations for the loss of lives" and that "We must pray for the most innocent of souls (the unborn). Heaven is crying because of the killing of the innocent." We appease the Lord's anger through prayer and sacrifice Our Lady had said to me. Man has strayed so far away from the Lord now with these senseless acts of abortion and terrorism. We must pray for a change of hearts.

The Rosary Group at my Parish played a big part prior to my pilgrimage. I was able to be free in relaying Our Lady's messages to them. I would tell them that we had first dibs so to speak on the messages from Medjugorje. We were doubly blessed because the messages that we received in Mineral Wells were eventually passed along to two visionaries, Mirjana and Marija from Our Lady. I also received other things from Our Lady that I passed along to the Rosary Group that didn't reach Medjugorje. Perhaps it will eventually.

These detailed visions were so vivid as I stated before; it felt as though I was literally transported to Medjugorje many tines. Most of these vivid visions transported me specifically to Apparition Hill where Our Lady first appeared in June of 1981. I could see myself walking along the jagged rocks as I made my way to spot that marked Our Lady's first sighting. I was *shown* many people kneeling there, deep in prayer. Our Lady would comment on this many times. Typically She would say that these were Her Children whom sought to *hear* Her, whom I would be sent to pass along Her Words. Many times I was given to *feel* these people's heartfelt prayers as well.

There were so many things that were *shown* to me in the first two months of 2019 leading up to my departure date in late February. There were also a fair amount of personal things that Our Lady passed along to me as well. These first two months of 2019 were intense. I will finish this chapter with Our Lady's message to Marija from February 25, 2019. I also received some part of this message beforehand. I was relieved that I did. I wanted to head into my pilgrimage with this *connection* to the messages and the visionaries in tact. I felt it was a perfect transition into my pilgrimage.

Feb 25, 2019

"Dear children! Today, I am calling you to a new life. It is not important how old you are, open your heart to Jesus who will transform you in this time of grace and, like nature, you will be born into a new life in God's love, and you will open your heart to Heaven and the things of Heaven. I am still with you, because God permitted me out of love for you. Thank you for having responded to my call."

Chapter 6: Week #1

February 27, 2019, the date of my departure finally arrived. My long awaited return to Medjugorje was at hand. Even though it had only been eleven months since I had been there, it felt like ages.

My mother had minor surgery in Ft Worth, Texas, the day before and so I made a stop at the hospital before I went to the airport. I was there for a couple of hours with my mother and some of my family members as I nervously anticipating my upcoming flight.

It was going to be two flights and a long bus ride to get to Medjugorje from Dallas/Ft.Worth but I was ready because I knew I would be in Medjugorje within twenty-four hours.

The first leg of my trip landed me in Frankfurt, Germany and I was little nervous after I arrived because the gate connecting me to my second flight to Split, Croatia, was still closed. The language barrier made it a little difficult to get to where I needed to go. It wasn't until and hour or so before the flight that the small security check point leading to the connecting gate opened. By that time, I spotted a priest walking up to the small security gate entrance. I walked to him and said, "are you Father Damien?" and He said he was. I knew from some information on the Stella Mar pilgrimage website that Father Damien Wee from Omaha, Nebraska, was going to be part of the trip. Father Wee was accompanied by one of his parishioners. Father informed me that there were only going to be ten of us on this pilgrimage. I was happily surprised because my experience with a small group last year was incredible. With a small group, one gets to know the rest of the pilgrims very well.

As we got by the security check, most of the pilgrimage group was there except for two who were coming to Croatia via another flight. Cimela Kidonakis was the only one I knew there.

When we arrived in Split, Croatia, we were met by a familiar face, Miki Musa. He recognized me and greeted me with a hug.

We all boarded a big charter bus and made our way to Medjugorje. We were all tired as we trekked along the beautiful Croatia coastline. Miki gave us a talk about the history of the area heading in Medjugorje. He said he would speak about Medjugorje itself when we got into Medjugorje. I dosed off during his talk that had some familiarity to it from the year before when I made the same trek.

My heart was beating fast with anticipation as we entered the familiar confines of Medjugorje. Seeing the two bell towers of St. James Church, all I could say to myself was "I'm finally here!".

The feeling was immediately different from last year soon after passing St. James as our charter bus made our way to Mirjana's pansion. The feeling last year was of excitement at this same point but I didn't really feel much of anything else as our small group unloaded and quickly had a simple early dinner.

Miki gave us a rundown of that evening's program and tomorrow's schedule. Some of the group if not all, made our way back to St. James for the evening's International Mass. There was Adoration shortly after Mass and I stayed a little while for that before heading back towards the pansion. I made a quick stop at the Blue Cross and prayed giving thanks to Our Lady for bringing me back to Medjugorje.

I was a little down as I expected to *feel* something grand, as I was back in the place I had longed to be. My room at Mirjana's pansion had a view of Apparition Hill and so right before bed, I opened the curtains and with this beautiful view, I knelt down and I began to pray and invoke the Queen of Heaven.

Our Lady quickly came and said, "You've done everything I've asked of you (leading up to this pilgrimage), now trust that I'm with you. When the Holy Angel came to me (Annunciation) I too was afraid (like I was a bit today) but I trusted in the Heavenly Father's Will. You too must trust (that I'm called here and being led)." She then said once again that I was to be with the group for a time. She concluded our conversation by saying that I must trust and be who She wants me to be for the "faithful." This was an incredible way to end this long day, with a vision of Our Lady in Medjugorje!

The next day, March 1st, was a grace filled day. At the daily English Mass in the Chapel that sits behind St. James, I began to *feel* something. It was like a switch was turned on within me and I was given to *feel* everything and *feel* everyone. I then immediately *felt* sadness and hurt and then during Consecration of the

Holy Eucharist, Our Lady gave me the first message for a fellow pilgrim from our group who was sitting next to me. Our Lady said to tell her that "she will receive her strength here (Medjugorje) necessary to take on what she has going on at home." Our Lady then said that this fellow pilgrim had answered the call to come here. I then *felt* this incredible confirmation (extreme chills throughout my body) from the Holy Spirit that this message was truly from Our Lady and that the *work* here in Medjugorje had begun. This confirmation was so powerful; that I got teary eyed. I definitely would have cried a lot more had I been alone. I gave this pilgrim the message on the way back to Mirjana's pansion. I gave her a little bit of my testimony especially of the *work*, as we made the twenty-minute walk back. She thanked me a couple of times, as she was truly a believer. She had big family issues and will definitely need this strength Our Lady spoke about to win her family back. I felt so different after this compared to yesterday.

Then after lunch, we had some free time and so I climbed Apparition Hill for the time on this pilgrimage. I finished praying a Rosary there and then Our Lady *sent* me to another person sitting there alone on one of the many white rocks sitting atop of Apparition Hill. I first asked this woman if she spoke English and she replied with "a little." Our Lady said that this woman was praying for her family and to tell her that, "She is listening." When I asked this woman if she was praying for her family, she said "yes, I'm praying for peace for them". I then told her what Our Lady had said and that Our Lady had her family within Her Immaculate Heart. I did the best I could in relaying the message and I hope this woman understood what had just occurred. When I had gotten up to go speak with this woman, I got up with no hesitation to my surprise and I *knew* at that point that the Holy Spirit was moving me.

I finished my second Rosary of the day at the Blue Cross. I *knew* that a lady I saw praying there was praying for her family and some big health issues. I just prayed for her from where I was in regards to her. Perhaps this was part of healing prayers I was sent to do as well. I *know* that this woman was sincere in her prayers and I *know* Our Lady was hearing her petitions as well. There were too many people around for a personal *message* to be given to this woman. Our Lady then said to me at this point, "many people come here asking for help with their families (conversions, health)." Our Lady continued saying, "that is what they ask for the most." We must completely trust in the Lord and Our Lady with our petitions for our families.

Being the eve of the Apparition of March 2nd, the group made plans to arrive at the Blue Cross early the next morning to get a good vantage point for the Apparition. Being familiar with what occurs during the Apparition from last year, I suggested where the best place to set up would be. Our spot ended up being on the opposite side of where I was the year before, just behind the statue of Our Lady. Last year I was up and behind Her right side and this year it was up and behind Her left side.

The Apparitions on the 2nd of the month usually occur around 8:30-8:45am local time. I arrived at the Blue Cross around 4:30am as it was cold and still dark out. The lights leading up to the top of Apparition Hill from the base were still on this early March morning. A couple of people from our group were already set up at our spot. We all began praying multiple Rosaries as the pilgrims began to fill the areas around us and below us as dawn broke.

I anticipated the Apparition with some excitement but not to the level of the previous year. The music was even a little different pre-Apparition compared to last year. Overall it just had different feel to me. The excitement from the group was visible but something internally was beginning to disturb me as the hour of the Apparition drew near. It was similar to what I felt the first day.

I began to feel that too much focus was on the visionary Mirjana and not on what was about to happen. I was *picking up* all the negative part of this whole Apparition experience. It affected me to the point that I hardly *felt* anything during the Apparition itself. I was expecting somewhat of a repeat of what experienced last year and I was disappointed that it wasn't. I believe some of this was my fault for allowing the negative to affect me the way it did. The positive things I did *feel* was the brief presence of Our Lady as Mirjana had her vision.

My thoughts were that perhaps I got caught up last year in being a first time pilgrim and getting caught up in the excitement of the Apparition.

The message to Mirjana on March 2, 2019, was as follows,

"Dear children, I call you 'apostles of my love'. I am showing you my Son who is the true peace and the true

love. As a mother, through the mercy of God, I desire to lead you to Him. My children, this is why I am calling you to reflect on yourselves, starting out from my Son, that you look to Him with the heart and that you may see with the heart where you are and where your life is going. My children, I am calling you to comprehend that it is, thanks to my Son, that you live - through His love and sacrifice. You are asking of my Son to be merciful to you and I am calling you to mercy. You are asking of Him to be good to you and to forgive you, and for how long am I imploring you, my children, to forgive and to love all the people whom you meet? When you comprehend my words with the heart, you will comprehend and come to know the true love and you will be able to be apostles of that love, my apostles, my dear children. Thank you."

When the group got back to the pansion, everyone was abuzz about what they had experienced. I was just waiting for the message to be posted to compare what was received by Mirjana to what I had received earlier.

When the official message was posted at the pansion, I quickly snapped a picture of it on my phone and read it thoroughly multiple times. It was definitely something I had received within the last week or so before arriving to Medjugorje. I even asked Father Wee what he thought the main theme was on today's message from Our Lady. I said to him, "do you think it's about mercy?" and he said yes. I asked him just to confirm to myself what I had received earlier was indeed today's message.

This was the only comfort I felt after the Apparition, knowing that I was still *connected* to Medjugorje in this way.

This internal *feeling* that was building peaked over the next couple of days after the Apparition. During the morning English Mass and the evening International Mass and all the time in between, all I could *feel* was the negative part of all the souls I was around. I *felt* pain, hurt, and the darkness of sins all around me. I *felt* souls who didn't want to be at Mass, souls who were just going through the motions so to speak and souls who were absolutely miserable. This wasn't that these souls I was *given* to *feel* weren't receiving anything by being in Medjugorje, this was just that I was *given* to *feel* and *know* why they were in Medjugorje in the first place. It was for healing, conversion and whatever else their souls needed. I just focused too much on the negative aspect and not on the beautiful graces that they were receiving. I was absolutely exhausted.

I went to Adoration in the Chapel, which they hold everyday and I prayed fervently for help and by God's infinite mercy, He heard my desperate pleas and He guided me to the Sacrament of Reconciliation. I went and stood in line for Confession right as the evening program started. I waited in line for about ten-fifteen minutes until it was my turn. There weren't that many people at that point standing in the multiple lines waiting for their confession. The priest hearing my confession was Father Wee. I was relieved that it was him for some reason. Perhaps because I was familiar and comfortable with him.

After I confessed my sins, I went into what I was feeling. I was able to tell Father Wee about the *work* the Blessed Mother had called me to .He said Our Lady didn't call me all the way over here to abandon me. He said "the evil one will try to do everything in his power to discourage me." I didn't even think about that during this darkness. Even though Our Lady warned me about it before the trip it had escaped me. Father then asked if I felt better at that point and I said that I still had a little "darkness" left. I then told him about the person who was called to chronicle the *work* that I was to do. He said all I can do is give that person the *message* and not take it personal if they reject it. He then said that the Lord is using me in powerful way to pray for souls and to trust in Him and Our Lady. This was the most incredible experience I've ever had in the confessional. I was in there for around forty-five minutes. The people, who were behind me in line, were no longer there. I believe there were multiple English speaking priests in the other Confessionals to hear their confessions.

I realized I had to pray for these souls whom I just *saw* darkness and not light. Mass had already started and so I proceeded to pray for all these souls at the large, beautiful Luminous Mysteries plaques located behind St. James Church and the outdoor altar. What an incredible peace I received from the beautiful confession and spiritual guidance from Father Wee! Thanks be to God! "Take one day at time" Father Wee had also said when I told him about my fears heading back home. In particular the fear of being stuck in the same old routine. I didn't want things to be the same even though what I was *experiencing* wasn't routine. I wanted things back home to be like Medjugorje because that's what I felt was going to happen with everything Our Lady had said to me all those years ago as I wrote about in my previous books.

The light returned in my soul and I once again saw the pilgrims with sympathy and empathy and not judgement.

Wednesday of that week began a little rough after the English Mass as I tried to explain to this person that Our Lady wanted to chronicle the *work* but this person was totally not in tune with what I was trying to explain. They retorted with a totally *out of left field* rambling. It was extremely frustrating to say the least. As long as I had been discerning this and to get the response I did, it really irritated me.

I prayed a Rosary on the way back to Mirjana's pansion to calm down. I was invited after Mass as well by other members of the group to go up Apparition Hill and pray a Rosary with them. I initially turned them down because of my frustration that had just occurred with the other pilgrim but I eventually decided to go and by God's infinitive Mercy, He allowed me to be used as Our Lady had intended.

The pilgrim who vexed me was also with us as we made the prayerful climb up this holy hill. I tried not to let this person being there bother me. By the time we got to the top of the Hill, we stopped once again to pray; Our Lady then *showed* me the intentions that all the pilgrims were praying for. One of the pilgrims from our small group later said that she could smell roses all over (she said the aroma was with me too). That was a beautiful confirmation that Our Lady was with us and letting me know what I was *receiving* was truly from Her.

I saw one of the ladies from our small group of pilgrims

praying in front of statue of Our Lady which marked the spot where She first appeared in 1981. By the prompting of Our Lady, She sent me to this woman to relay a *message* that I had *received* for her. I was once again sitting on one of the many rocks atop Apparition Hill observing and *listening* when the Blessed Mother *moved* me to speak. I went to the pilgrim and I asked if I could pray with her and she said "yes." I prayed aloud for a bit calling on Our Lady and praying for this woman as well. I then told her that Our Lady is listening to her and I said to give all her fears (new job, family, etc) to Her. This woman teared up. Through my peripheral vision, it seemed that the vexing pilgrim took a picture of us praying at that moment and of me delivering the *message*. The pilgrim did technically *chronicle* the *work* at that moment and so that came to pass as Out Lady had asked albeit it was just for a brief moment. The pilgrim that I had prayed for, asked me when we reached the bottom of the Hill by the Blue Cross why I went to her and I told her that Our Lady had told me to. This woman began crying once again knowing truly that the Queen of Peace was hearing her heartfelt prayers.

At dinner that night, we all gave our nightly testimony of what our grace was for the day and both pilgrims, the woman I prayed for and the woman who smelled the roses gave testimony to what happened on Apparition Hill earlier that day. Truly inspired by the Holy Spirit, I was able to give a strong testimony about Our Lady. I implored the group to continue to respond to the Blessed Mother's call out in the World. I made a promise to keep praying for them. I added if they ever needed any special prayers or fasting on my part for any intentions they may have in the future, that they could call upon me at any time for that and I would most graciously oblige.

A few nights earlier I was able to give my testimony to three other pilgrims from our group at Mirjana's after we returned from the evening program and dinner. I spoke to them about my life and the *work*. I felt this comfort with them and that's why I shared my reason for being in Medjugorje. They seemed very sympathetic and intrigued. I was very thankful that I got to share my testimony with them. Sometimes I feel that I'm hiding something if I don't share in particular situations especially in a place like Medjugorje. I don't feel that I have to share with everyone though. Most all of the second group of pilgrims that came later and half of this group weren't aware of my testimony. I understand it may not be for everyone.

We had Mass at Mother's Village a couple of days earlier. Mother's Village is an orphanage that was started by Father Slavko Barbaric to take in all the children who became orphans because of the Bosnian War in the early 1990's. The Mass was straight out of the dream I had a month before my pilgrimage. Both in the dream and in real life, Miki said that our group had to celebrate Mass. I did the first reading for the Mass like in the dream. I purposely volunteered to read, as I *knew* this was what I was *supposed* to do. I even had to lift the book of readings up as I did in the dream because it was difficult to read because of the lighting. There were also multiple Altars there like in the dream as well. I was keenly aware what was happening as events unfolded that morning. I believe all this occurred because Our Lord was showing me that I was on the right path here in Medjugorje even though the darkness was still palpable at that point. This gave me a little bit of joy knowing I was on the right track.

The group's last full day was Ash Wednesday. We all went to Mass that morning. It was special beginning our Lenten Season in Medjugorje. The day was bittersweet because the group, whom I had gotten very close to, was leaving. I knew I was going to be on my own for awhile before the next group came in about a week's time. After the evening prayer program we all gathered at a place to eat. The group was fasting being Ash Wednesday and so they ordered pizzas to eat at midnight. Their bus was to arrive at 2:30am. I stayed up with a few of them who decided not to sleep and wait for the bus in the big dining room at the pansion. We reminisced about the incredible week we all had. As much that happened in the first week, it was hard to imagine that I still had two weeks left. I was going to have to change hotels during the second part of my pilgrimage. I already knew this prior to my trip. The hotel was just up the road towards Apparition Hill and off to the right. The hotel was the Two Hearts Hotel. I stayed there the second part of the week during last year's pilgrimage as I wrote about in the first Chapter. Cimela had come as well to see the group off during this very early hour. She was staying in the apartment close to St. James. Cimela had planned to stay in Medjugorje for several more months to complete work on some other projects they had going. The bus finally arrived and we saw the small group off and then I finally headed back to bed anxiously awaiting what Our Lady had in store for me next.

Chapter 7: Week #2

Thursday morning came and the second part of my pilgrimage had begun. I was tired by the time I got up for breakfast but I knew I had to continue the *work*. Three pilgrims from the first group, including Father Wee's mother and aunt, stayed an extra day as they were from Singapore. Their friend Carol also came along with them. I ate breakfast and dinner with them that last day but I was mostly on my own. They left early the next day. I went to morning Mass that Thursday morning and then I rested some in my room at the Two Hearts before lunch.

Refreshed after a short nap and lunch, I climbed Apparition Hill once again. I prayed a Rosary specifically to be *given* souls to pray for and to relay Our Lady's words to them. I struggled a bit to climb, as I was still full from lunch. At the top of the Hill, by the statue of Our Lady, I once again sat atop of the many whitish rocks and I prayed to *see* whom Our Lady wanted me to approach. I started to feel some pain in my stomach from the food from lunch and so I was uncomfortable and I knew I couldn't stay long. Our Lady did speak to me and said, "Thank you for your sacrifice. Offer some prayers (three Hail Mary's) for all the souls here. I will answer their petitions as they made a sacrifice themselves to come here." There were about ten-twelve people or so atop of Apparition Hill and so I prayed for them as Our Lady asked. As I made my way back down, a large group was making their way up. I believe Our Lady wanted these souls who were already at the top to be prayed for specifically because these souls made the climb with a genuine intention. Sometimes it *felt* to me that some people climbed Apparition Hill as part of a *checklist* thing to do in Medjugorje. I also prayed for all the souls who were going up though. Right at the First Joyful Mystery plaque close to the bottom of Apparition Hill, an older Italian woman was sitting way across from the Plaque. I waved at her as I passed her as I descended and by the prompting of the Holy Spirit and of Our Lady, I turned around and I went back up to pray with her. I asked her if she spoke English and this Italian woman who was probably in her late 70's nodded no. This was the furthermost point I believe she was going to make it up Apparition Hill. I said to her in some very broken Italian, "let's pray." We prayed a Mystery of the Rosary together. She prayed in Italian and I in English. We went back and forth praying. I *knew* Our Lady wanted me to pray with this woman. It was a very beautiful moment. She was so gracious for me having stopped and prayed with her. She gave me a hug and a kiss on the cheek. I *know* Our Lady made everything turn out as it did on the Hill this day. At that point I could *feel* all the beautiful prayers in the village at that time. The power of the Holy Spirit was in full effect. What an incredible, incredible feeling this was. Praise be to God! The second part of my pilgrimage started off with a bang.

As Friday began, a lot of what Our Lady had said to me and what She had *shown* me, had come to pass in the first eight days. From the relaying Her *words* to Her children to the *feeling* drained from the *work*, to the praying for a lot of souls, it all came true. Even the dream of the Mass that I had prior to my trip came to pass. In a small way the fellow pilgrim who was to chronicle the *work* did come true as well.

Some of the homilies from the many Masses I attended also confirmed the *work* I was doing. Like Father Max, who celebrated or co-celebrated the morning English Mass during my time there, saying on that Friday morning about sacrificing for the love of God and sacrificing for our neighbor. He added, "In that sacrifice we can save souls." Father Wee also said the same thing as well saying that Our Lord will bring souls to us to pray for and if not, that's going be on us, on our souls.

I was praying for as many people as I was able to do so by God's grace. I did *feel* death on Friday morning as well as I made my way to Mass. I prayed a Chaplet of Divine Mercy for the soul(s). I prayed multiple Rosaries for many intentions on this day. I also went up Apparition Hill again for the fifth time and I offered a Rosary for the people going up and for those who were atop of the Hill and also for Our Lady to point *the way* like the day before.

I was then *given* to approach a German woman. She was praying for family like I had said to her when I spoke to her. She didn't understand much when I tried to get into the details Our Lady had given me for her. I hope and pray that she did get the gist of the *message*. Our Lady said that this woman was praying for her son, for his conversion. She said, "prayers of mother are very powerful. I saw my Son suffer and die and I understand the pain of a mother." She wanted this woman to continue to pray and offer the Holy Rosary for her son's conversion. I tried to convey the message the best I could to this woman who was around her late

50s or early 60s. I had been praying for the opportunity to approach her but there were people around her. I didn't want an audience for this private *message*. Our Lady finally cleared a path for me. The aroma of roses came as the path cleared for me. It was Our Lady confirming to me that I was to be Her *voice* to this woman. I didn't feel much peace after this as this death *feeling* continued.

Right before the evening Mass, I heard Our Lady say not to be troubled that She is with me in this *work*. I was extremely drained by the time I went back to the Two Hearts pansion after dinner. This day was filled with prayer and sacrifice for souls. I received news from home that one of cousins suffered a stroke the day before. I *received* back to back dreams about his family, my cousins, earlier in the week. They were very present in my prayers because of the dreams. I believe the Lord was showing me that they were going to need major prayers. As of this writing, my cousin is well on way to recovery now. Thanks be to God.

The next day was mostly a day of rest. I just let Our Lord and Our Lady take over. I needed to rest. I was given this advice by some friends who were familiar with what was happening concerning the *work*. After morning Mass, I went to sit in St. James Church and prayed asking Our Lord for help once again.

One thing that did occur during morning Mass was that I heard some Irish nuns behind me telling the Irish priest who was celebrating Mass, about a fellow nun who passed away Thursday in Northern Ireland. They had just found out that she had passed away in her sleep. Was this one of the souls I was given to *feel* (death) the day before?

I don't believe in coincidences and so for the me being in a position to hear of this passing and *feeling* death the day before, I believe this was part what I *received* in order to pray for this soul who was about to die. God is Mercy!

After lunch and after a break, I prayed a Rosary at the Blue Cross for my physical healing of the Type 1 Diabetes that I was diagnosed with back in 2010.

As I walked to the evening program, I prayed for all the prayer intentions that many people had asked me to pray for as I took the long ways path to St. James. I went to Adoration in the Chapel and I let everything go. I called upon Our Lady immediately and She came and said that She desired that I rested this day so I can begin "anew" tomorrow as She put it. She said "many souls come here and receive their conversion" because of Her coming to Medjugorje then in turn (She) leads them to Our Lord. Many come as well but do not change because of their hardened hearts. We need to see with the eyes of our faith.

Perhaps that's why some people don't change because they seek a *miracle*. I prayed hard once again asking for help, because I can do nothing on my own and at that moment, I heard the words of Our Lord. He said as I was praying for my healing and other intentions, that "I will receive my healing." He didn't say when, but I gathered it will be tied in to Our Lady's Apparition. Which Apparition? Honestly I don't know.

I prayed fervently to be cleansed of anything that was

not of Him. I believe this physical healing will occur when it's time. The Lord was reaffirming His promise to me in granting me this healing as I wrote about in my previous book.

What an incredible hour of Adoration! The Lord knows my heart and my needs and He will not abandon me. Lord I Love You!

On Sunday March 10th I climbed Apparition Hill after breakfast in thanksgiving for everything that I had been blessed with so far on this pilgrimage. It was a beautiful morning to climb. There were a few pilgrims atop of the Hill as I finished my Rosary. I then went to English Mass, which is 12pm on Sundays. It was a perfect way to start this day.

I had lunch at the Two Hearts pansion and I spoke to Lucy, who is the owner of the pansion along with her mother Marija. I really needed to talk with someone, as I hadn't really conversed with anyone since the group had left. Lucy was really understanding of the *work* as she has her own *gifts* from Above. Lucy said that her mother Marija was also blessed with many Charisms as well and so she was totally open to everything I told her that early Sunday afternoon. She had some very good insight on what I was experiencing and some great testimony of her own through her years in Medjugorje. I was very grateful for her help that day. The Lord knows when we need consolation in midst of trials and tribulations.

I climbed Apparition Hill once again after my long talk with Lucy for souls and for the *work*. There were many more people in Medjugorje this day as many new groups came in. I met and spoke briefly with some young people from a Canadian group this morning before Mass and I ran into them on the way up as well. I sat for awhile praying and observing and waiting on Our Lady to come. She finally spoke and said "many people come (up) here and ignore my Son. I'm here to lead them to Him but they just forget Him (there's a big Crucifix just above where Our Lady's statue is). It pleases me when souls come to Him first before they come to me". I know I must do that from now on every time I climb the Hill.

I then saw a woman near the Crucifix whom I *knew* I had to relay a message. Our Lady cleared a path and I approached this woman who appeared to be Italian and seemed to be in her 50's. She said she spoke a little English when I asked if she did. Our Lady had given me to tell her that She was happy that She was there. She also called this woman her daughter, which I also passed along. Our Lady also said that She wanted this woman to continue praying the Rosary because She hears her prayers in this way. This woman took this *message* very graciously with a hint of tears in her eyes. She thanked me and I made my way back down.

There was also another young man who was in his late 20's whom I wanted to approach as it *seemed* he was discerning the religious life. I just prayed for him, as I wasn't *sent* by Our Lady to speak to him. Perhaps I was just "given" to *know* his reason for being there.

At the Fifth Joyful Mystery plaque on the way down, some men from the Cenacolo, the rehab center for men, had a woman (Latina) in a seated platform as she prayed. The Cenacolo men carry those who can't climb

Apparition Hill on a platform. I wanted to go pray for over this woman but I just stood behind them and prayed for her. Then halfway down, there was another Cenacolo group with a man with an oxygen pack but who was walking just in front of the seat of the platform. I just prayed for him as well from where I was. I know this was something else that Our Lady wanted me to do as well, as part of the *work* but I had use some caution in these particular situations. The attention may have been directed at me had I just interjected myself in the middle of these small groups, and not on the person who needed prayers as it was getting a little crowded heading up Apparition hill.

While I was observing and praying the *feeling* of something else to do there in Medjugorje was with me. It felt like something big. It felt like this part of the *work* is not to be the main focus now. I later understood what this would mean.

One thing that happened at Mass this morning, with all the new people in town, was that I *felt* this *feeling* of hope and excitement which was a welcomed *feel*. Thank you Lord! I had this peace all day and at the International Mass that night it continued. It felt like after all that happened in Medjugorje this week with the darkness and such, that this trip was turning out to be an incredible, unbelievable pilgrimage.

I learned after dinner that night that an Ethiopian Plane crashed today shortly after takeoff and 157 people perished. This was the feeling of death I had. It had *felt* like a terrorist attack or a massacre of some sort but I *knew* it was a multitude of souls. The more this death *feeling* lingered that I wrote about a few days ago in my notes, the more it felt like a multitude of souls. I expect to see something on social media the day before with news of something tragic happening. I know that Our Lord had mercy as I prayed for these souls many times (Chaplets of Divine Mercy) before theirs deaths. I believe that's one of the reasons this death "feel" was gone this morning and why the peace was in the forefront.

The next day ended up being a rough day. I had a dream of Father Wee praying over a dead body and sprinkling Holy Salt, Holy Water and Holy Oil on the body, which was still on a gurney. He wanted me to assist him in praying over the body. The area we were at seemed to be near the old Grand Theater in my hometown of Mineral Wells. The theater had long closed down. In the dream that area along that part of town, was revitalized which is starting to come true in real life. I woke up feeling the affects of the dream. The peace was gone from the day before. Later that day I read on social media that a body was found in my hometown down that same road from my dream in a grassy area. Was this the dream? I believe it was. I found out later that the body that was found was of a man who committed suicide. He was someone that I knew from one of the jobs that we do as part of janitorial services back home. I had prayed for this soul before he perished. Whatever despair he felt at the time of his death, was conquered by Our Lord's Divine Mercy. This *death feeling* was with me all day despite all the prayers.

After Mass this morning I once again prayed in St. James and then prayed very fervently back at the pansion as I started to feel ill. I believe I picked up a stomach bug or something. I prayed for healing for my whole body. I ended up eventually buying antibiotics for it.

I did make it to Adoration in the Chapel before the evening prayer program. I had very limited interaction with anyone today which made things harder spiritually. It also rained almost all day and so that added to the way I was feeling. I was only able endure this day by God's grace and by Our Lady's intercession.

I know the evil one had a field day with me on this day but I offered this day for souls and so in the end God won.

Right before I went to sleep. I received news of a second death from back home. The mother of this young woman who I know passed away. I always pray for this young woman on a daily basis when I pray the Chaplet of Divine Mercy. My prayers include her family as well. With these incredible heightened *feelings* this second week in Medjugorje, I was *given* to pray for this young woman's mother before she passed as well. I know the Lord had mercy on these two precious souls from my hometown.

I woke the next day feeling better despite my sleep being disrupted mainly because of thinking about these two souls who passed away. The awesomeness of God's Mercy still astounds me after all these years of praying for souls.

I went to morning Mass and prayed about thirty minutes before Mass began and I also prayed a couple Rosaries after Mass. I visited Father Slavic Barbaric's tomb, which is located in a cemetery behind St. James Church and the outdoor altar and I prayed for his intercession.

I went up Apparition Hill as well on this cold and windy day and there weren't many pilgrims up there. I offered a Rosary for everyone's intention who were going up this day. Our Lady accepted this for these souls as She said She would answer their intentions (according to God's will) because of the added sacrifice of these souls going up in this weather. I couldn't *feel* very much in terms of being *given* to *know* what the few people who were up there were praying for. Our Lady seemed to say as I also felt, that this part of the *work* was done except for a few exceptions. The *work* will continue at home in "spreading of Her messages" as She put it, the messages of Medjugorje. She said that I did what She had asked of me. I knew had to continue to pray for discernment on what She had said this day.

I finished the day with Mass once again in the evening and with two more Rosaries. What a difference on how I felt from the day before. I was eagerly awaiting the next group who were due in the next day. I had already been praying for them even before they arrived.

Chapter 8: Week #3

The day came when the second group was to arrive. The second week in Medjugorje seemed like an eternity after being pretty much alone. I admit that halfway through these three weeks here Medjugorje that I was ready to go home but I knew I had to complete my *work* here. I never would've thought that I would have this feeling of wanting to go home being at a place that I longed to be. I was worn out.

The group was to arrive in the early afternoon like my 1st group did when I first arrived. I started my day as I had the previous two weeks, with breakfast and morning Mass. I climbed Apparition Hill one more time after lunch and then I patiently waited for the new group of pilgrims to arrive. I had waited about an hour in the lobby of Mirjana's pansion when the charter bus arrived with the new group. I helped unload the luggage from the charter bus as I saw many tired but excited faces. I felt out of place, as it appeared that this new pilgrimage group had already made a connection with each other. I saw a couple of familiar faces though. Miki, our guide, had arrived shortly before the bus did. I was happy to see him. Cimela arrived with the new group as she had gone to meet them at the airport in Split, Croatia. They scheduled an early dinner that day for the exhausted travelers shortly after their arrival and so I wasn't able to make it to the evening program at St. James.

After dinner though, I help lead some pilgrims to the

Blue Cross, as many of the pilgrims were first timers. There were some that had been to Medjugorje before though. It was dark out as we made our way to the Blue Cross. The tired faces made way to an excitement once again as they realized they had finally made it to Medjugorje. I made some brief conversations with some of the pilgrims before I made my way back to the Two Hearts pansion for the night.

The next day, March 14th was a busy day. Once again being a *veteran* of Medjugorje. I helped lead the pilgrims to morning Mass through the fields from Mirjana's. There was an air of excitement at Mass and in the village as an influx of pilgrims had streamed in. I fed off that excitement.

After morning Mass we had the orientation by Miki. I sat and listened to this familiar talk as though it was my first time listening to it. I was happy. I guess I was just relieved to be in a set program that I was familiar with and also that I wasn't alone.

I prayed a lot for myself at the Blue Cross and at Mass that morning and at the evening Mass. I knew this third week was to be different for me and that's why a lot of the focus this first full day with the group was for my own soul. I did *feel* and *sense* something this day but I wasn't sure what it is.

I prayed very fervently during the night Adoration at St. James, which was beautiful. It made me feel a lot better compared to how I felt coming into this last part of my pilgrimage. I did *feel* death earlier in the day though, which I prayed a Chaplet of Divine Mercy for.

The theme this day for me that was reiterated at Mass and through the homilies was, "ask, seek and knock". Our Lord knows what I'm praying about here in Medjugorje. I was specifically praying this day for a renewal in spirit and body. I was praying for another transformation so to speak into whom Our Lord truly wants me to be. I knew that I had to keep praying on this during my final week. A note about yesterday's climb to Apparition Hill prior to the group's arrival, I did *smell* a light fragrance of Roses, indicating that I was discerning correctly that this last week in Medjugorje was to be personal.

I got to know some of the group better today and especially this evening after Mass and then Adoration. I sat with a family from Houston, Texas, at dinner and we had plenty of time to converse. It was a blessed day.

I slept well heading into the second full day with the group. After breakfast we all made the familiar walk to morning Mass. These walks provided an opportunity for me to get to know my fellow pilgrims on very personal level. Each day and night of the pilgrimage, walking back and forth from the pansion to St. James, provided us all an ample opportunity to bond with each other.

We all climbed Apparition Hill (tenth overall time for me) after Mass and right before lunch. On the way up with the group by the Cross that marks the spot where Marija had an Apparition of Our Lady when She gave the message of "Mir,Mir,Mir... "(Peace,Peace,Peace...), Miki spoke about Father Gabriele Amorth, the famous late exorcist, and immediately the dream that I had the night before made sense. In the dream, I'm in a mansion and I'm telling an Indian boy who was around fifteen years old who didn't believe in God about Father Amorth. I was talking to him in behest of his mother. I was telling this young teen about Father Amorth's book *An Exorcist Tells His Story*. I also mentioned the documentary on a streaming service that I saw called *The Devil and Father Amorth*. I told him that the director of *The Exorcist* movie from 1972 made the documentary. So when Miki brought up Father Amorth I got excited. Then a woman from the group mentions his books when some of the group where asking Miki about Father Amorth. I kept quiet, as I *knew* this had to take place for a reason. A very short time after this I found out why.

After the Fifth Joyful Mystery plaque as we heading towards the statue of Our Lady atop the Hill, the young Indian boy from the dream was there with a couple of men. One of them asked me where I was from. I had seen them around Medjugorje during the previous week. These two connections from the dream made me smile. I believe it was pointing to what was about to happen at the statue of Our Lady.

I prayed the Rosary going up with the intention to be given the grace to *know* what it was I was *feeling*. It was also to *know* what Our Lady was still asking of me. As I sat there at my familiar spot on one of the rocks surrounding the statue, I prayed on this. I invoked Our Lady and She came! She came floating down from Heaven as She did to the visionaries so many years ago. It was like I could *see* them as they were then back in 1981. She said that Her Son had granted me many (incredible) things in terms of *receiving* in regards to Our Lady but that I still needed my faith to grow on this last part of the pilgrimage. This was what the purpose of the last part of my pilgrimage. I needed my faith to grow in order to serve as the Lord has called me (healing etc.) to. It was clear in terms of why my healing and other things that I had been praying for extensively hadn't been answered.

The *other* things I've been given to do, which my previous writings go into, I had been given great faith to accomplish but my faith on this part, the personal petitions, was really lacking. I felt this great peace after this. I was answered on what this last part on the pilgrimage was truly for! Thank you Mother!

I meditated on these things and I prayed for an increase of faith during the evening Mass. The incredible feeling right before Mass that this pilgrimage had once again become something otherworldly came to me. Praise be to God!

The other thing from the day before came to pass today tragically. As I wrote about the day before that I *felt* death, came true in the massacre in New Zealand this day. Forty-nine people were killed in a terrorist attack (mosque). It was "One of the nation's darkest day's" as one of the headlines read. This was what I was given to *feel* yesterday. The Lord's Divine Mercy once again prevailed over evil in the end.

I gave Lucy, the owner of the Two Hearts copies of both my books this day as well. I pray she reads them and receives something from them. I *felt* that this was something I was supposed to do as part of this long pilgrimage.

There was one other personal petition that I asked Our

Lady about this particular day and the Blessed Mother replied with "(to go with) whatever is in your heart". I pray that the Lord had borne *this* on my heart. What an incredible day! To have Our Lady come to me in this incredible holy place of Medjugorje is something I can't even describe. It's very humbling.

The next day, March 16th, we had Mirjana's Q&A. There were a lot more people during this session compared to my first group's session. We had a big Korean group join us. The dining room at Mirjana's pansion was absolutely packed during this talk. I didn't really try to get an up close seat because I wanted to have some of my fellow pilgrims from our group to sit close to Mirjana who was sitting against the wall where we typically sat for our meals. This was going to be my third time attending the Q&A session in about a year's time. The way it ended up being arranged in terms of seating, I ended up with a close vantage point to Mirjana anyway. I didn't ask any questions like I had the year before but one of the things Mirjana answered echoed what Our Lady had said to me the day before on Apparition Hill. The question was about faith. I don't remember how the question was exactly worded but Mirjana's response was clear. She told the pilgrim who asked the question that the pilgrim had greater faith than she did. The reason being that she (Mirjana) didn't have to have faith to believe that Our Lady is appearing because she physically sees Her. The pilgrim, through great faith, believes Our Lady is appearing without seeing Her. This was confirmation on what Our Lady had spoken to me about my own faith.

I took of a picture of a young Korean Priest who was part of the group that came in for the talk. He was sitting by another Korean priest who was sitting next to Mirjana during the session. Mirjana always invites priest to sit by her during these talks. The young priest, whom I captured, had this smile that summarized the whole pilgrimage experience for many of us. It was a smile of thankfulness, amazement and of being incredibly blessed by being in Medjugorje all rolled into one.

We had lunch right after the session and I didn't feel too well afterwards. I *felt* death again and I ended up prayed a second Chaplet of Divine Mercy for that. When I was walking to the Chapel to go to Adoration, the St. James Church Bell was ringing once again marking a death in the village. Perhaps this is what I *felt* but as the night progressed the *feeling* got stronger. Was it more World tragedy coming? I had already prayed about and so I just left it to God's Infinite Mercy.

Adoration did make feel better a bit before the death *feeling* peaked that night. I continued praying for an increased faith and for my personal petitions. Perhaps being in Medjugorje was making everything I was *receiving* really in tune for me in a big way because I was in a place that was so spiritual. I headed to bed early as Miki had the group scheduled to up Cross Mountain very early the next day before Mass.

After an early breakfast on the morning of March 17th, we left to go climb Cross Mountain. It was a little tougher climb than two weeks ago when I went up with the first group. I guess my legs were worn out at this point. I was walking an average of around seven miles a day and having climbed Apparition Hill ten times already; it had taken a toll on my legs. I could also tell that I had lost some weight as some my clothes were fitting loose.

After Mass at 12pm we had some time on our own before the evening program. One thing I was *given* to do right before Mass though was that I was able to give the small group of pilgrims from Canada whom I met during my second week a gift. I knew from my first conversation with them that they were scheduled to leave Medjugorje on March 18th. They weren't going to be able to stay for Mirjana's Apparition. A couple of days before, I *received* this inspiration to given some blessed Rosaries. These Rosaries were blessed by Our Lady during the Apparition of March 2nd. When I saw the leader of the Canadian group with a couple of teenagers from the group, I went up to them and I presented them a pack of Rosaries. I explained to them how Our Lady had blessed them during the Apparition. The young teens eyes quickly widened with joy and surprise as I presented them the Rosaries. They graciously thanked me. A few minutes later, a couple of more teens from their group sought me out and graciously thanked me for the gift. It brought me joy knowing that they were able to have something special to take back home with them.

We had some time after Mass on our own and so I rested back at the pansion and contemplated my long stay in Medjugorje. It was hard to believe that my trip was close to the end.

After the evening Mass and dinner with some of the group, I was able to talk to Jim, one of the pilgrims who came with his wife Krista and two of their three daughters from Houston, as we made the walk back to the pansion. I gave him some of my testimony during our long walk and talk. He had some great advice for me. He also offered a good take on why I was *receiving* the *messages* from Our Lady in advance of Mirjana's and Marija's messages. He said how the Gospel writers had different takes on the same story of Christ; Our Lady was just doing the same thing with this. This made a lot of sense. Jim has a good understanding of the Charisms we all receive through the Holy Spirit and through his experience with his prayer group at his Church. It was a blessing to talk to him. I felt good as I headed to bed.

Some of us from the group had made plans to go out to the Blue Cross early the next day to get a good spot for Mirjana's yearly March 18th Apparition. I was hoping and praying that this Apparition would be better spiritually for me than the one from March 2nd with the first group.

I left the Two Hearts pansion to go to The Blue Cross- around 5:45am the next morning as I was a little worried that our spot behind the Cross would be taken. A few pilgrims from our group were already there and so I joined them. The rest of the group came shortly after and some a bit later after they had breakfast. We had a big enough area there and so those who arrived a little later had room to be by us. The Apparition was to take place around 1:45pm and so we had almost 8 hours to go when I first got there. We prayed 4 Rosaries before the official Rosaries began with the music and loud speakers. We took turns going down to pansion for food and for restroom breaks.

As the pilgrims filled in and as the time approached for Mirjana to arrive, the *feeling* of evilness was strong. It was a little strange to *feel* this. There were a couple of *screamers* coming from below our area. They weren't visible at this point as the Blue Cross and surrounding area were packed with pilgrims. The memories of the dream I had of the *false* Apparition came to mind. Perhaps this was part of it coming to pass, meaning the evilness being present. This *feeling* then made way for the presence of the Holy Angels. Their presence was very clear to me. This was what I felt the year before.

The anticipation of Our Lady's coming was building. As Mirjana finally arrived and knelt in front of the Blue Cross and began to pray, the presence of Our Lady became even stronger. I *felt* Her coming some time before Mirjana did, as this *incredible rush* would come in spurts. When Mirjana reacted to Her coming (I had prayed invoking her beforehand) I could *hear* Mirjana speaking to her. It was unclear what she was saying as she was speaking Croatian but I heard Our Lady's words in English "I'm your Mother the Queen of Peace" and then I heard her mention Her Son and then I heard Her mention peace. I then *saw* Her speaking to Mirjana as I did last year. It was just as strong as last year but I was by God's grace, more in control and *aware* of everything around me. It was an incredible moment to say the least. I tried to focus on Mirjana like I did last year, trying to tap into her feeling and I was *given* to *feel* some of what she felt. It was mostly the joy that Mirjana was feeling. Then Our Lady said to me "I'm about to depart, continue your mission when you go home" and then I *felt* the Queen of Heaven leave and about a second later, Mirjana reacted visibly by almost putting her head to the ground as the Apparition ended for her. This sequence gave me my confirmation that Our Lady was truly with me on this breathtaking day!

The multitude of pilgrims at the Blue Cross that day had no clue on what I was granted from Heaven that day. I felt humbled.

Many from our group *felt* many beautiful things this day as they testified later. One of them was really touched by the day's events and couldn't quite wrap his head around what he experienced. Another from our group pointed out the sun breaking through the clouds and it forming a Cross. I saw it as well. He said that he saw Our Lord on the Cross as well. Another pilgrim saw a ring/circle descend down from the Sun and when it reached the ground Mirjana reacted to Our Lady's coming.

I was able to absorb a lot of beautiful feelings there at the Apparition site but after a late lunch and then praying another Rosary with some of the group at the Luminous Mysteries plaques behind St. James, I felt awful. This feeling *felt* like death and so I prayed a Chaplet of Divine Mercy on way back to the Two Hearts. I couldn't stay for the evening program and for dinner afterwards because of the way I was feeling. I came to realize by God's grace that I also absorbed a lot of hurt and deep spiritual pain as well during the Apparition. It was a rough feeling to put it mildly. To be *open* to the beauty of this day's events also left me *open* for the opposite.

The Apparition from this day was just as powerful for me as the year before and a far cry from what I experienced on March 2nd with the first group.

The message from Our Lady to Mirjana was something She had already spoke to me about. This made ten messages in a row now and five messages in a row from Marija's messages.

The feeling this night made me feel as though I may never come back to Medjugorje again. Only Our Lord knows such things. Was this *feeling* something or just a byproduct of what I had *picked* up this day? It's all in the Lord's Hands and in His Divine Will.

The *death feeling* I felt two days ago was the Netherlands shooting that was all over the news this morning that occurred on the Tram that claimed three people's lives. What an up and down day.

The message to Mirjana Soldo from March 18th is as follow.

Mar 18, 2019

"My children, as a mother, as the Queen of Peace, I am calling you to accept my Son so that He can grant you peace of soul - that He can grant you that which is just, which is good for you. My children, my Son knows you. He lived the life of man, and at the same time of God: a wondrous life-human flesh, divine Spirit. Therefore, my children, while my Son is looking at you with His eyes of God, He penetrates into your hearts. His tender, warm eyes are looking for Himself in your heart. My children, can He find Himself [there]? Accept Him, and then the moments of pain and suffering will become moments of tenderness. Accept Him, and you will have peace in (your) soul - you will spread it to all those around you - and this is what you now need the most. Heed me, my children. Pray for the shepherds, for those whose hands my Son has blessed. Thank you."

The next day, our final full day in Medjugorje, was bittersweet in some ways. I was excited and more than ready to go home but the *feeling* from last night was still on my mind.

During this last day we attended a talk from Father Leon which was great. That made me feel better. Everyone loved him. Then we all attended Mass right after, which was beautiful as this was the Feast Day of St. Joseph The Mass and receiving Our Lord in Holy Eucharist further picked up my spirits.

We then had lunch and we were able to see Mirjana once again as she helped serve us lunch. Someone had commented how quickly she had recovered from the Apparition on the 18th. I also heard that she was also spry the day before the Apparition, which was also unusual. Mirjana had given a talk earlier to a room full of Italian pilgrims as we ate breakfast. It was fascinating to hear her as she spoke Italian. The combination of my knowing Spanish and having learned some basic Italian words, I was able to understand quite a bit. To see her once more during lunch was a beautiful grace on our final day. We were able to say goodbye to her.

I went to the evening program that night and I prayed a final Rosary for the intentions that I had gathered throughout my three weeks in Medjugorje. The whole group had a final dinner together at Colombo's, which is right by the Church, which was very nice. Sean, Cimela and Jessi Hannapel (the three members of Stella Mar Films) were all there with us. They gave us a screening of their new fascinating documentary *Where There Is Darkness* the night before which was incredibly generous of them.

The final dinner was a great way to end our pilgrimage. I was able to share some of my testimony with a couple of more pilgrims as we walked back to the pansion. They shared some of their experiences with me as well.

Our Lady's *work* and my *mission* will continue to unfold as time goes on. I honestly don't know when I will return to Medjugorje. I did start to miss it some this final night but I'm ready for the *next* thing. Mary Queen of Peace Pray for Us! Jesus, I trust in You!

Chapter 9: Post-Medjugorje 2019

As we headed out early Wednesday morning towards the airport in Split, Croatia, I left with a sense of gratitude for the grace I was given in serving Our Lord through Our Lady.

Several pilgrims from our group asked me to pray for some special intentions for them before we left Medjugorje.

As we arrived in Munich, Germany, from our flight from Split, most of the group quickly parted ways, as we had to take different connecting flights heading back to the US. I followed two brothers from our group, John and George Baker, as we had the same connecting flight. The two brothers towered over me as we walked through the airport to reach our connecting gate. We had some time before departure and so the brothers decided to get a light meal beforehand. I joined them as we all sat at a small table next to the small restaurant.

We all talked about the pilgrimage a bit along with some other small talk. I wanted to ask George, the younger brother who was in 60's I believe, about what I overheard him saying during our time at the Blue Cross prior to Mirjana's Apparition. He had said during that time that he had cancer and that his prognosis wasn't too good. The doctors had given him something like a two-year survival timeframe. When I asked him about this in Germany, George went into great detail about his condition. I come to find out that John his older brother, also had cancer but it wasn't nearly as dire as George's. John has had his cancer for years. By the inspiration of the Holy Spirit and by the *work* that Our Lady had called me to, and Her call for me to continue my *mission*, I asked them if I could pray for them. At first they thought we were going to pray a Rosary, but I said that I wanted to pray for healing for both of them. They graciously accepted my request. We all held hands as we were still seated and I proceeded to pray for healing for both of them in the middle of the airport in Munich, Germany unbeknownst to all the travelers passing by. The Holy Spirit truly guided the prayers in that moment as I could *feel* the Spirit moving throughout us. I hope and pray that God's healing and mercy will touch the Baker brothers.

After a bus ride, three flights and an overnight stay with my brother, I finally made back home to Mineral Wells. I went to morning Mass with my brother the day he took me back home. That was a great way to get started to what Our Lady had called me to do when I got back home, *to be Her voice*.

After I got home, I gave some testimony to some of my family on what transpired in Medjugorje. When we had our weekly Parish Rosary that Sunday, I gave the group some testimony as well. I *received* a vision during our Rosary and Our Lady spoke to me once again. She appeared to me as Our Lady of Medjugorje. She said what I was given to do Medjugorje was laying the groundwork for what to is occur here in my hometown of Mineral Wells. The connection I received to Medjugorje via the *messages* is to give legitimacy here in Mineral Wells. She asked if I wanted to continue the *mission* and I said yes without hesitation. I believe Our

Lady asked this because She wanted my "yes" to be of my own will and for it to be truly to be a resounding yes. My yes was a "Yes!".

It appears as though that the two pilgrimages from last year and this year's, the *work*, the visions, all of it was for Her *coming here*. It's why She said I needed to increase my faith to be able to *work* when I got back home to Mineral Wells. We're to be a Medjugorje West so to speak. We're to be an extension of Medjugorje. Perhaps not a grand scale, but as a holy place where pilgrims come and experience Our Lady's presence without having to travel halfway across the World. It seems that through all these years Our Lady was guiding me until the time was right. It did feel different coming back home this time compared to last year. Maybe it's why I felt that I might not see Medjugorje again because my *mission* as She says, is here now. I know I have to pray for more discernment on this. It all seems to make sense now after all these years of *receiving* pieces of this plan from Our Lady.

A few days later Our Lady spoke once again about my *mission*. The vision that night was of Our Lady as the Queen of Peace as She announced Her appearance by that greeting. Her words were exceptionally clear this night. She said that I was free to ask Her my questions that I had this particular night. I asked about the connection to Medjugorje once again and She said "you're (we) an extension of Medjugorje. Many can not travel such long distances to see Me there. You will be my voice to those who are seeking me (like the *work* in Medjugorje). My children seek answers and you will speak to them (on Her behalf). Call upon me and I shall come and speak (through me)." She mentioned the

Prayer Garden and Chapel where these visions will continue to take place. I could *see* the Prayer Garden as this vision was taking place very clearly. I asked her to repeat it all and She did (the main points). I asked if She will call me to Medjugorje again and She said in time, but my task is here (for now). Our Lady said that She would bring the souls here when I asked how will they know that She is *here*. Our Lady continued speaking saying that my "mission" would be greater than *work* that I was given to do (in Medjugorje)". I know that I must continue to pray for discernment on this! Queen of Peace pray for us!

The next appearance of Our Lady took place that next Sunday at our weekly Rosary. The Rosary was held in Chapel and it was different in terms that I told the group what Our Lady had told me what the *mission* is now, and how we're connected to Medjugorje. I relayed all this to them before the Rosary started.

There were more people tonight as Our Lady came as Our Lady of Medjugorje. I was given to *see* Mirjana very clearly but I saw her as though she was facing me but looking up towards Our Lady as she is during an Apparition. This type of vision usually signals that a message that I have already received will be an upcoming message during Mirjana's monthly Apparition. What Our Lady said at the beginning was something like "the world is taking many souls away from my Son." This was like a combination of hearing this upcoming message to Mirjana and hearing Her message to us at the same time. The Blessed Mother said we needed to consecrate our families (especially our children) to Her. We needed to make sure "our house" was clean in order to help our family (children). We will take account to

Our Lord if we didn't lead them to Him, Our Lady continued saying. We need to make sacrifices (fasting etc.) for them, for their conversion. I was given to *feel* pain and hurt tonight. I believe a lot of the message was aimed towards certain member of the Rosary group as I was given to *know* that it was. One of the ladies this night commented later how powerful Our Lady's presence was tonight. Our Lady had said that she would bring souls to the Rosary and based on all the people there this particular night, She is. There was a point this night where the *feelings* and prayers of everyone was getting to me but by God's grace I was able to back off *feeling* them all the way. It lingered for a bit after the Rosary. It also *felt* as though that there is something that Our Lady is asking or trying to show me with the visionaries, specifically Mirjana. Perhaps it's a message from Our Lady? She also mentioned during the Rosary about praying for "the shepherds" (the priests) and also how the evil one is pulling families apart (something to that effect). There was a lot that was going on all at once during this vision. This night marked a new beginning in the path that Our Lady has us on.

The next week during the Rosary, I was given to begin the *work* in terms of being Our Lady's voice to certain souls whom She wanted to communicate with.

The vision this night during the Rosary in Prayer Garden was very powerful. We began this new journey by incorporating the chorus of the hymn Ave Maria in-between the Rosary Mysteries. We also made the period between the Second and Third Mystery longer to give more time for Our Lady to speak. This all set up Her coming.

She came in this brilliant light in which She appeared to be floating and She was dressed in all white. I asked Our Lady about a particular member of our group who earlier had asked me to inquire about something she was praying for. I told this group member earlier to get closer to the front where the statue of Our Lady is during the *period* when She typically arrived.

Our Lady said to this member that they had a choice to accept their illness for the rest of their lives for the conversion of souls specifically for this member's brother and for others. If this member chose not to sacrifice, their healing of this auto-immune disease that they have would be healed in time.

I told this person after the Rosary what Our Lady had said about her request. Later they messaged me saying that it was a hard message that was given and that they did pray for healing at the time but then said to Our Lady that they would accept it for the conversion of their brother. This was confirmation that the message I gave them was truly Our Lady speaking to us.

This vision this night was powerful enough for me not to sense anyone who did get close to me during the period Our Lady made Herself present. I'm typically aware of my surrounding during Her *coming*. I almost broke down crying a couple of times with the powerful presence of Our Lady.

During this very long vision, I also asked the Blessed Mother about my nephew Marcos, who was sixteen at the time. Marcos wanted to receive confirmation from Our Lady on what he is supposed to do in his life. His spirituality is way beyond that of his peers and probably beyond a lot of adults as well.

I immediately *saw* Padre Pio there in front of him along with Our Lady. Our Lady said Marcos needed to "follow Padre Pio's example on how to suffer. To suffer for souls, for conversions, for healings." He needed to study Padre Pio in a way.

Marcos has a treasure trove of sufferings to use for this as he's had multi open-heart surgeries. Marcos was born with major heart issues. Marcos is a walking miracle despite all his surgeries and his past health issues. He's a *normal* teenager in terms of appearance.

During the vision Our Lady also had this burning light like an orange, yellowish glow where Her Immaculate Heart is. This light is the burning love She has for us, Her Children.

The last thing I *saw* was Mirjana and I asked Our Lady about it. It's a future *thing* involving her Our Lady said. I believe it's a message that Our Lady has for her. It's something that needs to be passed along. I received the details of the *message* during the week leading up to our weekly Rosary. It's a personal message and so it just for her. I know I must continue to pray on this. The time will come when it will be transmitted to her.

What a night! We were very close to what Our Lady was asking of us on how we are to conduct these beautiful Rosaries.

The subsequent weekly Rosaries and visions of Our Lady came with more *answers* to those who were seeking it. These advance messages that matched the

Medjugorje visionaries messages continued as well. Part of me thought that they would stop as soon as my *work* was done in Medjugorje but they didn't. How long will this continue? I honestly don't know.

It's been a blessing to be able to help people in the way that Our Lady has called me to. I pray in time that She will continue to bring souls as She said She would. I know that on my part, I have to be obedient and spiritually ready to *receive*. I know that my *duties* are not just limited to the *work* of Our Lady. The Lord has sent me multiple souls to pray for before their passing including one of my cousins from Mexico. I know that this part of my *work* is always present. Sometimes it all feels like it's all nonstop but the Lord grants me consolation and rest when it's needed. It's not much of it but it's very welcomed and I'm very grateful for that.

The friendships that were made with all three groups during my time in Medjugorje has also been an incredible blessing. Some of them have really been helpful in terms offering prayers and advice. All in all, I've been beyond blessed with this life I've been granted. I don't know if these three books I've written have done justice to Our Lord and Our Lady's incredible miracles that have taken place in my life.

I hope and pray that the testimony given in my writings will benefit souls on their own journeys. I pray that whatever results from this particular book that it will ultimately show Our Lady's great love for us all, Her children.

Queen of Peace, pray for us!

Acknowledgements

I would like to give thanks to the Lord God for the grace of allowing me to write this third book. Without Him, it would've not been possible. I would like to give thanks to the Blessed Mother for calling me and guiding me on this beautiful journey.

I would like to thank all those involved in helping me on this spiritual journey as well. Your prayers and spiritual guidance have been greatly appreciated.

I would like to give thanks to the people and to the pilgrims of Medjugorje. Their inspiration and genuine love for Our Lord and Our Lady have been extremely edifying.

I would like to thank Stella Mar Pilgrimages and Croatian Mir for an incredible pilgrimage experience during my twenty-eight days in Medjugorje.

I would like to thank my family, my Rosary group and all three-pilgrimage groups, whom I had the pleasure in experiencing Medjugorje with.

I would like to thank Melissa Garcia and Mirella Navarrete for their input on this third book. I like to Marisol Sosa, Jim Coppedge, Krista Gibson and Tom Van Hoven as well for their friendship and prayers.

I also would like to thank Jim Coppedge for the proofreading and his input for this book.

Marian Prayers

The Angelus

The Angelus is a short practice of devotion in honor of the Incarnation repeated three times each day, morning, noon, and evening.

The Angel of the Lord declared to Mary: And She conceived of the Holy Spirit.

Hail Mary, full of grace, the Lord is with thee; blessed art thou among women and blessed is the fruit of thy womb, Jesus. Holy Mary, Mother of God, pray for us sinners, now and at the hour of our death. Amen.

Behold the handmaid of the Lord: Be it done unto Me according to Thy word.

Hail Mary, full of grace, the Lord is with thee; blessed art thou among women and blessed is the fruit of thy womb, Jesus. Holy Mary, Mother of God, pray for us sinners, now and at the hour of our death. Amen.

And the Word was made Flesh: And dwelt among us.

Hail Mary, full of grace, the Lord is with thee; blessed art thou among women and blessed is the fruit of thy womb, Jesus. Holy Mary, Mother of God, pray for us sinners, now and at the hour of our death. Amen.

Pray for us, O Holy Mother of God, that we may be made worthy of the promises of Christ.

Let us pray:

Pour forth, we beseech Thee, O Lord, Thy grace into our hearts; that we, to whom the incarnation of Christ, Thy Son, was made known by the message of an angel, may by His Passion and Cross be brought to the glory of His Resurrection, through the same Christ Our Lord. Amen.

Magnificat of Mary

My soul proclaims the greatness of the Lord,
my spirit rejoices in God my Savior
for He has looked with favor on His lowly servant.

From this day all generations will call me blessed:
the Almighty has done great things for me,
and holy is His name.

He has mercy on those who fear Him
in every generation.

He has shown the strength of His arm,
He has scattered the proud in their conceit.

He has cast down the mighty from their thrones,
and has lifted up the lowly.

He has filled the hungry with good things,
and the rich He has sent away empty.
He has come to the help of His servant Israel

for He remembered his promise of mercy,
the promise He made to our fathers,
to Abraham and His children for ever. Amen.

Memorare

Remember, O most gracious Virgin Mary that, never was it known that anyone who fled to thy protection, implored thy help, or sought thine intercession was left unaided.

Inspired by this confidence, I fly unto thee, O Virgin of virgins, my mother; to thee do I come, before thee I stand, sinful and sorrowful. O Mother of the Word Incarnate, despise not my petitions, but in thy mercy hear and answer me. Amen.

The Hail Mary

Hail Mary, full of grace,
the Lord is with thee.
Blessed are thou amongst women
and blessed is the fruit of thy womb Jesus.

Holy Mary, Mother of God,
pray for us sinners
now and at the hour of our death.
Amen.

Jesus, I Trust in You!

www.ingramcontent.com/pod-product-compliance
Lightning Source LLC
La Vergne TN
LVHW041232080426
835508LV00011B/1170